FINE
FURNITURE MAKING
AND WOODWORKING

FINE FURNITURE MAKING AND WOODWORKING

Geoffrey Endacott

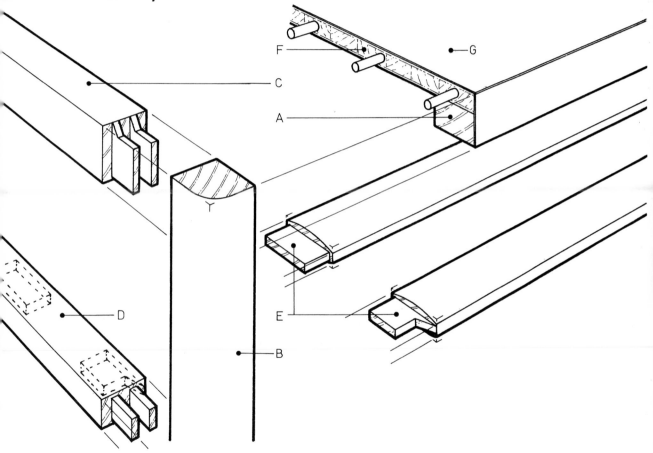

Sterling Publishing Co., Inc. New York

Library of Congress Cataloging in Publication Data

Endacott, G.W.
    Fine furniture making and woodworking.

    Bibliography: p.
    Includes index.
    1. Furniture making—Amateurs' manuals. 2. Woodwork—
Amateurs' manuals. I. Title.
TT195.E5   684′.08   81-85026
ISBN 0-8069-5458-2   AACR2
ISBN 0-8069-5459-0 (lib. bdg.)
ISBN 0-8069-7610-1 (pbk.)
ISBN 0-7153-8389-2 Great Britain

Published in the United States by Sterling Publishing Co., Inc.
Two Park Avenue, New York, N.Y. 10016
Published in Great Britain by David & Charles (Publishers) Limited
Brunel House, Newton Abbot, Devon TQ12 4PU England
Distributed in Australia by Oak Tree Press Co., Ltd.
P.O. Box K514 Haymarket, Sydney 2000, N.S.W.
Distributed in Canada by Oak Tree Press Ltd.
c/o Canadian Manda Group, 215 Lakeshore Boulevard East
Toronto, Ontario M5A 3W9
Manufactured in the United States of America

Table of Contents

PART II

Foreword

As author, illustrator, photographer, designer, and part publisher of *Fine Furniture Making and Woodworking*, I have attempted to create a book that is both informative and fun to read. It has been written with several goals in mind: to be an instructive guide to those who have never made articles from wood; to satisfy the appetites of those who have knowledge of the subject, but have long given up hope of finding a book that both instructs and challenges; to offer a diversified and intriguing range of projects that will appeal to woodworkers at all levels.

I believe that all these goals have been accomplished, and hope you will find in *Fine Furniture Making and Woodworking* a knowledgeable and entertaining passport to a very rewarding hobby.

GEOFFREY ENDACOTT

Introduction

Why do woodworking, and why make your own furniture? Initially, there are two myths I must expose. First, there is the notion that making one's own furniture will always save one money. Unfortunately, this is not true, for a single item cannot be made as cheaply as one that has been mass-produced. If you want low-cost furniture, then you must look for furniture that has been mass-produced and is offered for sale in stores and through newspaper advertisements.

Second, there is the notion that one can with some effort turn one's home into a palace or castle. I have dreamt such thoughts as this, but after twenty-five years of woodworking I still do not live in my castle. The reason is that I can neither work with sufficient speed nor find the time that the work requires: In short, it is humanly impossible. If you want your dream house to become a reality, then you would do better to earn the money so that you can employ people to build a house for you.

What then are the benefits of doing woodworking? For me, one reason lies in construction, for I enjoy thinking of new and exciting ways of putting wood together so that it is stable, works well, and looks good. Woodworking is, after all, a kind of three-dimensional chess game, and involves quite a lot of visualization. (Part II will show you how to carry out this design process.)

Another benefit is the feeling of pride that can be derived from making one's own articles. Much can be said for mass-production, which has helped raise the standard of living in many countries; however, the person who makes his own articles—those that cannot be mass-produced—is forging his own individuality and creativity into something that will provide many years of practical use. Such articles are called "one-offs," or "individual pieces."

Can you make a sideboard that fits in the alcove of your house; a coffee table that fits in front of the French windows; a built-in unit for your small kitchen so that the food can be prepared on top, the utensils stored underneath, and the doors do not get in the way? You'll be able to tackle these jobs, and many more, after reading this book.

As you read, you'll note what appears to be a set size for the items you want to make. Don't be dismayed by this. The sizes listed are given to help the beginner. If you are confident that what you are doing is correct, alter the sizes to suit your requirements. After all, this is what woodworking is all about—making things that you want the way that you want, bearing in mind the limitations of your materials, skills and equipment.

If you wish, you can stamp your initials and surname into your work. Metal stamps for this purpose are available at your local tool dealer.

I hope you come to enjoy working with wood. It is a material that is fairly easy to work, and yet is sufficiently firm to make a durable article. Everyone knows that Chippendale chairs are as good today as when they were made more than two hundred years ago, so there is no reason why the articles you build today should not last your lifetime and the lifetime of your children and grandchildren. After that we cannot be certain. But I am certain that if you want to make an article that will last, then not only do you have to construct it well, but you also have to give it spirit so that successive generations will not want to destroy it.

So far I have mentioned the durability of wood, but not the color or the grain. These two features appear with just a little effort. They are the spin-offs from working with wood, so try to use them wisely. Sharpen your plane and set it to remove paper-thin shavings. Make even strokes with the plane so that the full color and the grain effect appear. I have not yet used words like red, pink, scented, sweetly scented, gritty, open, and silky because I do not see the need to characterize all woods; determining which wood is better suited for a particular task is something you're better off finding out for yourself. Take a sharp plane and see how much enjoyment planing a piece of wood can bring.

ADULT EDUCATION

If you are as yet unsure about taking up woodworking as a hobby, then I suggest you approach your local education center to find out if adult education classes are available, and at a time of day that is convenient for you. The main benefits of attending a class are: 1) this is the least expensive way of practicing woodworking, and 2) you have the advice of an instructor—as good as this book may be, the advice of an instructor has the edge over the printed word.

A WORKSHOP AT HOME

Some readers are unable to attend an adult education center, and some may prefer to work on their own. Let us consider the problems in trying to find a place where woodworkers can work on their own. It needs to be somewhere 1) where dust and noise give least offense to other people, 2) where work can be left overnight for the glue to dry, 3) that is well lit—preferably by daylight—and with controllable ventilation, 4) that is dry, 5) that can be heated in winter, and 6) that has at least one electric power outlet.

I have some friends who temporarily solved the problem of finding a workshop by using an empty bedroom in their house. However, it was not long before the family grew and another use was found for the room. This may not happen to you, but it is unusual if guests do not arrive at some point and you are prevented from using the empty bedroom as a workshop. If you are very lucky you will have a basement in which you can work.

I have solved the problem of finding a workshop by erecting a shed in the garden (fig. 1). The shed measures 10 ft (3 m) × 8 ft (2.4 m), and it has 7-ft 6-in (2.3-m) headroom at the front that reduces to 6-ft 6-in (2-m) headroom at the back. This shed was bought factory-made, as it was cheaper than building it myself. It has walls that are made of western red cedar, and the roof is made of pine boards that are covered with heavy-duty roofing felt. The floor consists of concrete slabs that are loosely laid over a sand base, with one large layer of heavy-duty plastic sheet (polythene) underneath the sand to act as a water barrier. I have placed carpet mats over the slabs to reduce any possible damage to tools that might fall from the bench; the carpet also helps to keep the workshop warmer. In the center of the ceiling there is an electric power socket, and fitted to the ceiling above the bench there is an electric light. Have the electric wiring carried out by a professional, and ask that the grounding (earthing) be checked.

The workshop I have just described has lasted me well for seven years and should have a long life ahead of it. One advantage of this workshop is that it is portable; should I move to another house, then I can take the workshop with me.

Fig. 1 Garden workshop: This is made from western red cedar. It measures 10 ft (3 m) by 8 ft (2.4 m) and has 7-ft 6-in (2.3-m) headroom at the front.

PART I
Tools, Techniques, and Materials

American/British Terminology

American terms used in this book appear first. Their British equivalents follow in parentheses.

absorbent cotton (cotton wool)
alcohol (white spirit)
backsaw (tenon saw)
bar clamp (sash clamp)
base frame (plinth)
bench dogs (bench stops)
block joint fittings (bloc joint fittings)
brads (panel pins)
burlap (wall hessian)
can (tin)
carcass (carcase)
casters (castors)
C clamp (G cramp)
clamps (cramps)
clear (cleave)
clothespins (clothes pegs)
dado (housing joint)
dressed (ready planed)
drive in the brads (tap the pins)
edge cross lap joint (deep halving joint)
electric cord (electric flew)
end rabbet joint (lap butt joint)
factory (works)
fibreboard (hardboard)
flathead screw (countersink screw)

grounding (earthing)
jointing (topping)
nail set (panel pin punch)
nail the corners (pin the corners)
plain rabbet joint (plain butt joint)
plane iron cap (curling iron)
plastic sheet (polythene)
plow plane (plough plane)
pocket cut (plunge cut)
rabbet (rebate)
rabbet plane (shoulder plane)
sandpaper (glasspaper)
set the brads (punch the pins)
sliding T bevel (sliding bevel)
spade bit (flatbit)
Stanley picture frame vise (Stanley frame cramp)
steel wool (wire wool)
3 corner file (3 sided file)
topping (jointing)
tow truck (breakdown truck)
trial clamp (trial cramp)
van (lorry)
vise (vice)
white shellac (white polish)

Hand Tools

Hand tools are much cheaper than machine tools and you can do nearly as many things with them as you can with machine tools, though of course your progress will be slower. If you are going to attend adult education classes you will not be required to buy any tools, but you will need to know quite a lot about them.

I enjoy woodworking tools as objects in themselves, and can soon find a reason for buying more. My great-grandfather was a master carpenter, and because interest in woodworking had skipped two generations in my family, I came to inherit his tools. These came protected with petroleum jelly, individually wrapped in newspaper, and sealed in two of my great-grandfather's tool chests. Now, when I buy a new tool, I feel I am adding to his collection.

I have taken a careful note of the tools that I use regularly, and this is the list that follows. I have further reduced the number of tools I think you need buy initially, and for that list see Appendix A.

A HAND TOOL SELECTION

THE HANDSAW (fig. 2, a)

The handsaw is used to cut large sheets of hardwood and manufactured boards into smaller pieces. You need a crosscut saw with a blade length of 22 in (560 mm), and with about nine teeth to every inch (25 mm).

THE BACKSAW (fig. 2, b)

The backsaw (tenon saw) is used for accurate bench work and cutting tenons. Ask for a backsaw with a blade length of 10 in (250 mm), and with about fourteen teeth to every inch (25 mm).

THE DOVETAIL SAW (fig. 2, c)

The dovetail saw is used only when cutting dovetails. It has fine teeth that are tedious to sharpen, so its use is confined to this one type of work. Ask for a dovetail saw with a blade that is 8 in (200 mm) long, and with about seventeen teeth to every inch (25 mm).

THE COPING SAW (fig. 2, d)

This saw is used when making curved cuts in wood of less than 1-in (25-mm) thickness. The blades break easily, especially when you are not used to this type of saw, so buy a spare packet of blades with the saw.

A BENCH HOOK (fig. 2, e)

A bench hook will hold your wood steady when you are cutting with the backsaw. The bench hook

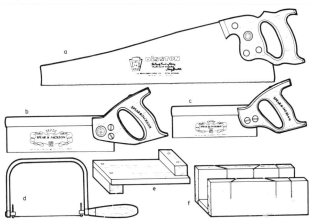

Fig. 2 Hand tools: (a) handsaw, (b) backsaw, (c) dovetail saw, (d) coping saw, (e) bench hook, (f) miter box.

also protects the top of the bench if you are a little bit wild when cutting with the saw. You can buy a bench hook made from beechwood, or you can make one for yourself by following the instructions given in Part Two.

A MITER BOX (fig. 2, f)

A miter box helps you to guide the backsaw when you are cutting on a 45° angle. This is particularly useful when cutting the corner joints for a picture frame. A spare piece of wood placed in the bottom of the miter box prevents the box from being cut as you saw through the picture framing. You can buy a miter box ready-made, or you can make one for yourself by following the instructions given in Part Two.

A MARKING KNIFE (fig. 3, a)

A marking knife is used to score a line across your wood at a place where accurate sawing has to be done. You can buy the traditional type of marking knife I have illustrated here, or you can do as I prefer to do, and that is to use the small blade of a penknife.

A STAINLESS STEEL RULER (fig. 3, b)

A steel ruler is used for the dual purposes of measuring and of checking that a surface is flat. To use the ruler for checking for flatness, hold your wood against the light and place the edge of the ruler on your wood; you will see how flat the piece of wood is by the amount of light that shines underneath the edge of the ruler. Ask for a stainless steel ruler that is 12 in (300 mm) long.

A PULL-PUSH TAPE (fig. 3, c)

This is very handy and very accurate.

A TRY SQUARE (fig: 3, d)

A try square is used when marking lines across the wood at right angles to the length of the wood. Ask for a 6-in (150-mm) try square. The size is

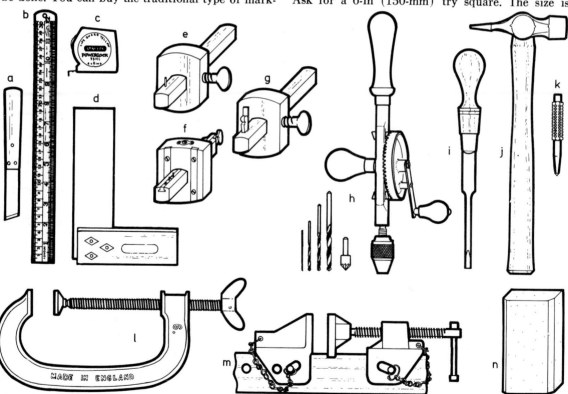

Fig. 3 Hand tools: (a) marking knife, (b) steel ruler, (c) pull-push tape, (d) try square, (e) marking gauge, (f) mortise gauge, (g) cutting gauge, (h) hand drill and drill bits, (i) screwdriver, (j) warrington hammer, (k) center punch, (l) C clamp, (m) bar clamp, (n) cork block.

measured along the underside of the blade and indicates the maximum width of material on which the try square can be used.

A MARKING GAUGE (fig. 3, e)

A marking gauge is used to score on the wood one line that is parallel to an edge of the wood. It marks only with the direction of the grain.

A MORTISE GAUGE (fig. 3, f)

A mortise gauge is used to score on the wood two lines that are parallel to an edge of the wood. It marks only with the grain. It is frequently used when marking out a mortise-and-tenon joint.

A CUTTING GAUGE (fig. 3, g)

A cutting gauge is used to score on the wood one line that has to be across the grain of the wood and parallel to one end of the wood. It is frequently used when marking out a dovetail joint.

THE HAND DRILL (fig. 3, h)

The hand drill can be more convenient to use than an electric drill because it is more portable, and can sometimes get into more awkward places than the electric drill. Good-quality hand drills have two pinion wheels—one turns the chuck and the other balances the pressure that is applied to the crown wheel. Ask for a double-pinion hand drill that has a chuck size of at least 1/4 in (6 mm).

Along with your hand drill you will also need some morse drills, so ask for a set of high-speed steel drills; you can use these later in an electric drill. You will need drills in sizes 1/16 in (1.5 mm), 1/8 in (3 mm), 3/16 in (5 mm), and 1/4 in (6 mm). You will also require a countersink drill so you can set the heads of flathead screws (countersink screws) flush with the surface of the wood.

A SCREWDRIVER (fig. 3, i)

At least one screwdriver is essential in your tool kit. Ask for a 6-in (150-mm) screwdriver to start off your tool kit, and buy others of differing sizes as you require them.

A CLAW HAMMER (fig. 3, j)

A hammer is used for inserting nails. It is also for tapping joints together; use a spare block of wood to hammer against, to avoid damaging your work. English readers are unable to buy the claw hammer, but must instead buy a warrington hammer. Ask for a claw hammer with a 14-oz (400-g) head.

A CENTER PUNCH (fig. 3, k)

A center punch is used to accurately position holes. Position the punch, then tap it firmly with a hammer. This will produce a small dimple in the surface of the wood.

A tool of similar appearance to the center punch is the nail set (panel pin punch). It is equally useful, as it helps to set the heads of small nails below the surface of the wood.

A C CLAMP (fig. 3, l)

A C clamp (G cramp) of 6-in (150-mm) capacity is useful for holding work onto the bench. It can also be used for holding small pieces of wood together while the glue sets between the pieces.

TWO BAR CLAMPS (SASH CRAMPS) (fig. 3, m)

Two bar clamps (sash cramps) with bar lengths of 42 in (1,070 mm) are used for holding work together until the glue has set. Clamp heads have been illustrated here, and these are attached to a hardwood bar that you make for yourself. It is cheaper to use clamp heads like this than it is to buy the type of bar clamp that comes ready-equipped with a steel bar. However, clamp heads on a wooden bar do not exert as much pressure as those on a steel bar.

Two bar clamps are the minimum requirement. I have three bar clamps, but there have been times when I could have used more.

A CORK BLOCK (fig. 3, n)

A cork block is inexpensive. It helps woodworkers grip a piece of abrasive paper firmly and apply more pressure on the abrasive paper.

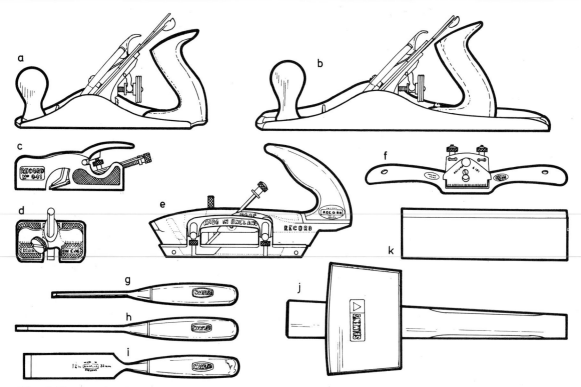

Fig. 4 Hand tools: (a) smoothing plane, (b) jack plane, (c) rabbet plane, (d) router, (e) plow plane, (f) spokeshave, (g) bevelled-edge chisel, (h) mortise chisel, (i) firmer chisel, (j) mallet, (k) oilstone.

THE SMOOTHING PLANE (fig. 4, a)

The smoothing plane is a plane of convenient size. It is used for shaping the wood, as well as preparing the wood to a smooth surface ready for polishing. Ask for a smoothing plane that is 10 in (250 mm) long.

THE JACK PLANE (fig. 4, b)

The jack plane is longer than the smoothing plane. The controls are identical to those on a smoothing plane. When the blade is set to remove a very fine shaving, the jack plane will plane a very flat surface. Ask for a jack plane that is 15 in (380 mm) long.

THE RABBET PLANE (fig. 4, c)

The rabbet plane (shoulder plane) has a blade that is as wide as the body of the plane, so it can be used for trimming directly against an edge. It is particularly useful when trimming the rabbets of joints. It may also be used for slimming over-thick

tenons—craftsmen say that tenons should be cut accurately with the saw the first time!

THE ROUTER (fig. 4, d)

The router is used to level the bottom of the dado (housing joint).

THE PLOW PLANE (fig. 4, e)

The plow plane (plough plane) is used for making grooves, rabbets, and tongues. It comes supplied with ten cutters of different widths.

THE FLAT-BOTTOM SPOKESHAVE (fig. 4, f)

The flat-bottom spokeshave is used for smoothing convex shapes, as well as smoothing slightly concave shapes. I have, on occasion, used this tool with the blade upside down; then it works more or less like a scraper.

CHISELS:

1) A ¼-in (6-mm) bevelled-edge chisel (fig. 4, g).

This is used for trimming between the tails of a dovetail joint.

2) A ¼-in (6-mm) mortise chisel (fig. 4, h). The mortise chisel can be hit with a mallet because the blade of the mortise chisel is much stronger than the blade of the bevelled-edge chisel. As its name implies, the mortise chisel is used to make mortises.

3) A 1¼-in (32-mm) firmer chisel (fig. 4, i). This is needed for general bench work.

THE MALLET (fig. 4, j)

The mallet is used mainly against the mortise chisel. Hitting the chisel with a mallet enables woodworkers to control the movement of the chisel. A good mallet is made from beechwood.

THE OILSTONE (fig. 4, k)

Woodworkers need an oilstone for sharpening chisels and plane blades. A good-quality oilstone will sharpen chisels and plane blades quickly and to fine edge, and will not wear out rapidly in the sharpening process. I have tried many oilstones, and have found none as good as the Norton India medium-grade oilstone. This is an expensive oilstone, but it is explained in Part Two how a wooden box can be made to protect the oilstone from damage and irregular wear. Ask for an oilstone that is 8 in (200 mm) × 2 in (50 mm) × 1 in (25 mm). You will need a light grade of machine oil, such as 3-in-One® oil, to use on the oilstone.

I have visited most of the tool factories in Great Britain. The majority of these factories are to be found in the city of Sheffield, which is in the north-east of England. Before the turn of this century the tool industry was little more than a cottage industry, with one man performing one process, then passing the work to his neighbor. The neighbor would always inspect the incoming work for quality before carrying out the next process. It has been said that the man who sharpened the chisels would throw the blades to the floor to make sure they had been hardened and tempered correctly. Presumably, any broken blades would not be paid for by him. No one wanted to get caught destroying tools.

Today, the work is still carried out in batches. At the Spear & Jackson factory the best-quality saws have their teeth hand-set by a craftsman. He hammers every alternate tooth in order to slightly bend all the teeth outwards. This produces the "set" on the teeth that prevents the saw from jamming in the saw cut. When the "setter" has completed a batch of saws he passes them to his neighbor at the bench, who hand-files each tooth in order to sharpen the saw.

I have also seen the Stanley factory where hammer heads are forged. If you live near a tool factory, write to ask if factory visits can be made, as a visit to a tool factory can be very interesting.

SHARPENING HAND TOOLS

CHISELS AND PLANE BLADES

Chisels and plane blades can quickly become blunt. Indeed, the harder and the more abrasive the wood the more quickly your chisels and plane blades become blunt. An abrasive wood such as teak can cause the cutting edges to become blunt in under five minutes. Sharpening is therefore a process that you must be able to carry out yourself. Here are the step-by-step instructions for sharpening all chisels and plane blades:

1) Apply some light machine oil to the surface of the oilstone.

2) Place the blade bevel downwards on the oilstone and raise the blade until it makes an angle of 30° with the surface of the oilstone (fig. 5). Rub the blade over the surface of the oilstone, making every effort to maintain the angle between the blade and

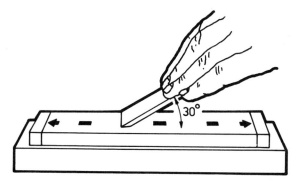

Fig. 5 Place the blade bevel downwards, and at an angle of 30° to the surface of the oilstone.

the oilstone at a constant 30°. Should you find it very difficult to maintain this constant 30° angle there are honing guides available from your tool dealer that will help you. As you notice from the illustration, I prefer to sharpen without a honing guide.

Continue to rub the blade over the oilstone until a burr has been formed all along the cutting edge. Feel for the burr with your finger (fig. 6).

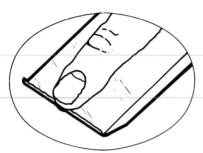

Fig. 6 Feel for the burr along the cutting edge.

3) Turn the blade onto its flat face and remove the burr by rubbing the first ½ in (12 mm) of the blade on the oilstone (fig. 7). It is very important that you do keep the blade flat on the oilstone, so bunch your fingers right over the end of the blade and press down heavily.

In order to remove the burr completely it is usual to have to revert to step 2 for a short period, and then revert to step 3. Repeating these steps for short periods will cause the burr to eventually break away, leaving the blade with a good, sharp cutting edge.

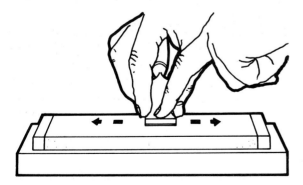

Fig. 7 Turn the blade onto its flat face and polish off the burr.

Fig. 8 Extreme corners of the smoothing plane and jack plane blades should be rounded with the oilstone.

When sharpening the smoothing plane or jack plane, the extreme corners of the blade should be rounded over on the oilstone to prevent their digging in (fig. 8).

When reassembling the smoothing plane and the jack plane, the plane iron cap (curling iron) should be placed within $\frac{1}{16}$ in (1.5 mm) of the cutting edge on the blade. Fully tighten the screw that holds these parts together, then replace them in the body of the plane with the plane iron cap (curling iron) uppermost. Put the chromium-plated cam plate on top of the plane iron cap (curling iron), and lock these parts in position by pressing downwards on the chromium-plated cam. Adjustments can be made to the blade by 1) moving the adjusting lever sideways until the blade cuts evenly, and 2) turning the adjusting screw until the blade removes only fine shavings from your work. A dab of oil on the bottom of the plane will make the job of planing quite easy.

The high-speed grindstone

After many sharpenings the sharpening bevel on any chisel or plane blade becomes enlarged; this makes the blade more difficult to sharpen. To make the job of sharpening easier, the sharpening bevel has to be ground at an angle of 25°.

Grinding is the coarse removal of metal. It is an operation that should be carried out on a slow-speed grindstone with the blade constantly cooled in oil or water. Not all of us can afford this expensive equipment, so we have to make do with a high-speed grindstone (fig. 9). Great care has to be taken to keep the blade cool; press the blade only lightly against the grindstone, and frequently remove the

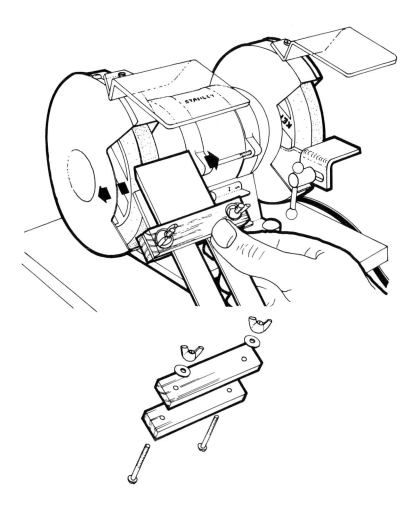

blade from the grindstone and dip it in cold water. If you do not take these precautions you will over-heat the blade and remove its sharpening properties.

Note in the illustration (fig. 9) that the tool rest has been tilted until the blade can be ground at an angle of 25°. This position has to be found on the grindstone by trial and error. A simple jig has been made to help grind the cutting edge square: Two pieces of wood, here, have been clamped together by bolts with the blade sandwiched between them. These pieces act as a guide when they are pressed against the tool rest.

Here is a list of regulations regarding the use of high-speed grindstones in the industry:

1) Grindstones are vitreous, so if you drop them they will crack. A grindstone that is cracked is likely to explode when run at its proper speed. For this reason, store spare grindstones carefully in a horizontal position between sheets of cardboard. Test a grindstone for soundness before running it on the machine; suspend the grindstone from a piece of string and tap the edge of the grindstone gently with a stick. A sound grindstone will produce a sharp sound, whereas a cracked one will produce a dull sound.

2) Cardboard blotters should be attached to both sides of the grindstone; outside of these are fitted large steel washers that are part of the machine.

3) The maximum speed of rotation for the grind-stone must be marked on the blotters, and this speed must not be exceeded by the speed of the machine.

4) The fixing nut must be tightened sufficiently, but without excessive pressure, to hold the grind-stone.

5) The tool rest must be positioned as close to the grindstone as possible.

6) Stout metal guards must be a part of the machine

to catch the pieces of grindstone should the grind-stone disintegrate.

7) The eyes of the operator must be protected by either a safety glass window on the machine or safety goggles.

8) Stand aside from the machine for half a minute after switching it on, in case the grindstone has an undetected flaw.

9) Apply the work gently and without bumping.

10) Avoid using the side of the grindstone.

11) Allow the machine to slow down naturally after switching it off.

SAWS

Saws in school workshops require sharpening once a year, but saws in the home workshop will probably stay sharp for several years. The sharpening of saws is a difficult process, and is made even harder by the infrequency with which this task has to be performed. Don't tackle this yourself; find someone in your locality who can sharpen your saws for you. You can locate your nearest saw-sharpening service in the Yellow Pages and the service columns in your local newspapers, or by asking your local tool dealer. If you still have difficulty write to the saw manufacturer, as it is likely that a saw-sharpening service will be provided at the factory.

For those who heed no warnings, live in a very isolated place, or like to tackle everything for themselves, here are the step-by-step instructions for sharpening a crosscut-type handsaw.

Sharpening a crosscut handsaw

The tools you require are an 8-in (200-mm) fine-cut flat file, a triangular file, and a pliers-type saw set.

1) Unscrew the saw bolts and remove the handle from the saw.

2) Devise a means of clamping the saw blade against the side of your bench so that the teeth project just above the surface of the bench.

3) Make a wooden holder for the flat file (fig. 10). The holder will enable you to run the file squarely across the saw teeth for the whole length of the saw. Run the flat file gently along the points of the teeth until every tooth has a small flat area where the

points should be. This process levels the saw teeth, making them even. It is a process known as jointing (topping).

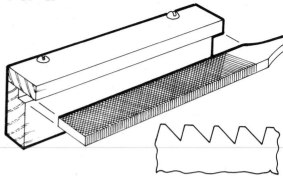

Fig. 10 Saw sharpening: A wooden holder enables you to run the file squarely along the teeth of the saw.

4) The next process, known as shaping, is omitted if the saw teeth are of a uniform size and shape. To carry out shaping, lower the blade of the saw at the handle end until the line of the saw teeth makes an angle of 16° with the bench top; this puts the back of the triangular file in the horizontal plane. By putting your thumb on the back of the file in order to maintain the file in the horizontal position, you will be filing the saw teeth at the correct cutting angle of 16° (fig. 11).

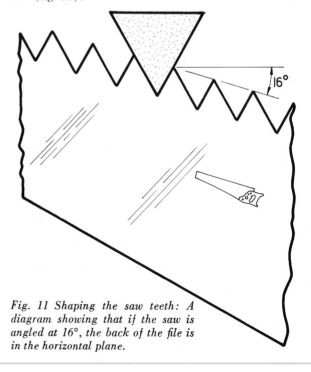

Fig. 11 Shaping the saw teeth: A diagram showing that if the saw is angled at 16°, the back of the file is in the horizontal plane.

5) The next step is to slightly bend the top half of each tooth outwards. This is a process known as setting, and each tooth must be bent in the opposite direction to its neighbors. Setting results in the teeth cutting a wider path than normal, and prevents the saw blade from jamming in the saw cut. The saw will often retain sufficient set for this step to be omitted. If setting is necessary, then you must first count the number of teeth points per inch (25 mm) of saw blade—include the points at both ends of the measured distance. Dial the number of teeth points onto the saw set. Apply the saw set to every other tooth (fig. 12). Make sure you continue to bend the teeth in the same direction they were bent previously; if you bend the teeth the wrong way they may break off! When you have completed one length of the saw, turn the blade around and set the remaining teeth.

6) The final step is to sharpen the teeth. This is done with the triangular file. Fix the saw blade low against the bench to reduce the amount of vibration, and have the saw blade positioned so that the handle end is initially on your right.

Use the triangular file in the horizontal plane, but turn the file so that the handle of the file is to your left and makes an angle of 70° with the saw blade (fig. 13). Make three slow passes with the file on the left of a tooth that is bent towards you. Transfer the file to the next tooth but one, and repeat the filing. Practice this on the teeth underneath the handle of the saw, as this is a little-used part of the saw blade.

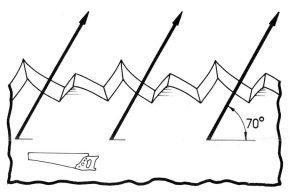

Fig. 13 Sharpening the saw teeth: Sharpen the alternate saw teeth with the file held in the horizontal plane, but at an angle of 70° to the saw blade.

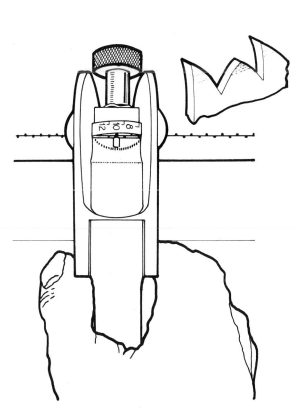

Fig. 12 Setting the saw teeth: Use a pliers-type saw set to slightly bend the tops of the teeth outwards in alternate directions.

When the filing of one side has been completed, turn the saw blade around so that the handle end is positioned on your left. Keep the triangular file in the horizontal plane, but turn the file so that the handle end of the file is to your right and makes an angle of 70° with the saw blade (fig. 14). Make three slow passes of the file on the right of a tooth that is bent towards you. Repeat this on the alternate teeth.

Filing should bring all the teeth to points, so check that this has happened. When you have finished, rub an oilstone twice along the saw on the sides of the teeth—not on the points—to even out the set.

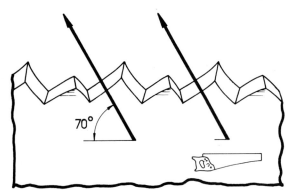

Fig. 14 Sharpening the saw teeth: Turn the saw blade around and complete the sharpening process.

Sharpening a backsaw

The backsaw (tenon saw) is sharpened in a similar manner to the crosscut saw. You can remove the handle from the backsaw (tenon saw), but do not remove the steel or brass back; this is part of the tensioning device for the blade, and it will be difficult to replace correctly.

Shaping of the teeth on the backsaw (tenon saw) is carried out at a 14° angle. You will need a triangular needle file and a hand lens in order to see that you are carrying out the work correctly.

Setting of the smaller teeth on the backsaw (tenon saw) may be difficult with the pliers-type saw set, so you may have to resort to using a hammer and a nail set (nail punch); try tapping the teeth against a chamfered block of steel. Remember that setting is only a slight bending of the top half of each tooth. The teeth are sharpened in a similar way to the teeth of the crosscut handsaw.

Sharpening the dovetail saw

The teeth of the dovetail saw are fine and tedious to sharpen, so avoid getting your dovetail saw blunt by using it unnecessarily.

When it comes to sharpening you can get away with filing the teeth straight across the blade at a 90° angle, instead of the 70° angle that is used with the crosscut saw and backsaw (tenon saw).

THE BENCH

Obviously, woodworkers need a good, strong woodworking bench that is fitted with a woodwork vise and bench dog (bench stop). The vise will help hold the wood when woodworkers plane an edge; the bench dog (bench stop) is a piece of wood or metal that projects through the top of the bench and prevents the wood from flying off the top of the bench when one side is planed. Clearly, the bench dog must be adjusted so that it is just below the surface of the wood and does not damage the cutting edge of the plane.

Kitchen tables do not make very good benches, as they are seldom rigid and do not have any accommodation for tools. A good woodwork bench is rigid, will have a recess so tools can be laid down without fear of their rolling onto the floor, and is probably made from beechwood, so it will last a long time.

You may have in mind the type of bench that you are going to use. You may not have much choice in the matter, but let us look at the Lervad 610™ wood-

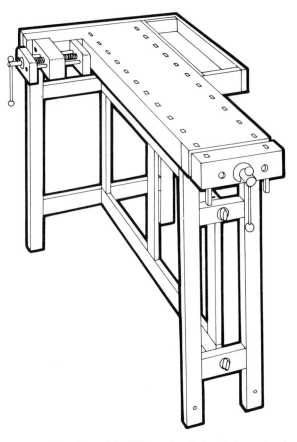

Fig. 15 The Lervad 610™ woodwork bench is made of beechwood.

work bench (fig. 15), which offers one possible solution. This bench is made in Denmark and is based upon a Scandinavian design. It is made from beechwood, and its top stands 32¼ in (820 mm) high. The top is 27 in (690 mm) wide, but it is narrower at one end; it's only 10½ in (270 mm) wide and takes up very little workshop space compared with other woodwork benches. The top of the Lervad™ bench comes fitted with three facilities for holding your work. First, it has a shoulder vise (fig. 16, a). Second, it has a full-width tail vise (fig. 16,

b). Third, it has a double row of slots for use with metal bench dogs (bench stops) (fig. 16, c). The bench dogs can be used in conjunction with the tail vise to provide a four-point hold that is useful for some operations.

Some people will find the bench is too low. The height of the bench is an important factor in the making of comfortable working conditions. I have raised my bench on wooden blocks from the floor so that the top is at chisel length—about 11½ in (290 mm) below my elbow.

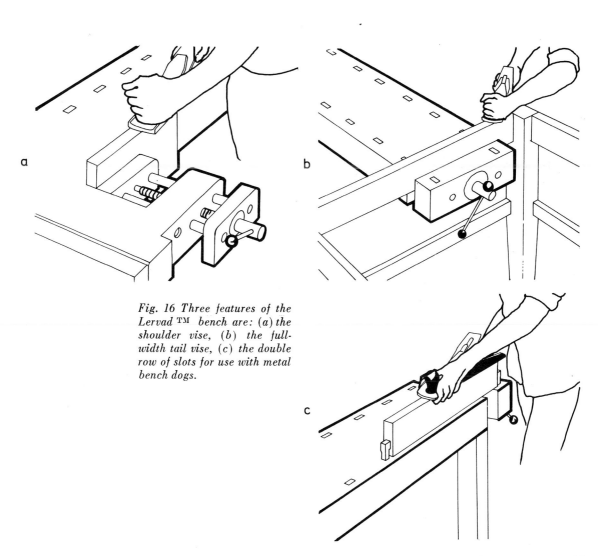

Fig. 16 Three features of the Lervad ™ bench are: (a) the shoulder vise, (b) the full-width tail vise, (c) the double row of slots for use with metal bench dogs.

Machine Tools

Some readers will find this section of little interest, while others will read it avidly. Machine tools are a subject of controversy, but I would like here to put them in perspective.

As a boy I visited the workshop where my great-great-grandfather and my great-grandfather had worked as carpenters. Since their time no one in my family had held any interest in woodworking, so I inherited their tools. There were two chests of tools. On opening the lids I found that each tool had been carefully smeared with petroleum jelly and wrapped in a sheet of newspaper by my late great-grandmother. I unwrapped each tool and took account of this treasure. Most of the tools were made from beechwood, which had now darkened with age. There were planes as long as a person's arm.

There were thirty moulding planes that looked alike, but each could produce a very different moulding from the others. There were spokeshaves, drills, and one very small plane that I could hold in the palm of my hand. In the workshop there were no machine tools, and there never had been any machine tools. All the work done in the workshop had to be carried out by hand.

Since the time of my great-grandfather, machine tools have come into woodworking. In the intervening years there have been controversial arguments about the merits of hand work and the merits of machine work. I suggest you write out a list of the advantages and disadvantages of working with machine tools, and the advantages and disadvantages of working with hand tools.

If you look closely at your list, you should find that the advantages of working with machine tools do not compensate exactly for the disadvantages of working with hand tools; neither do the advantages of working with hand tools compensate exactly for the disadvantages of working with machine tools. Obviously, the concept of machine-tool woodworking is different from the concept of hand-tool woodworking.

Most of us are already more familiar with the use of hand tools than we are with machine tools. In order to develop your understanding of machine-tool woodworking I want you to consider the following points:

1) Any machine tool is expensive, and you can often perform the same operation with less expensive hand tools. Would you, therefore, be better investing your money in several hand tools, rather than in one machine tool that can only perform a limited number of operations?

2) All machine tools are more noisy than their nearest hand-tool counterparts. Is the noise the machine makes likely to disturb you, and are other people likely to object to the noise?

3) Machine tools are more dangerous than hand tools. Are you prepared to find out how to operate each machine tool safely?

4) Because machines are power driven, some people erroneously believe that machine tools do not require sharpening. Are you prepared to give the time to sharpening and adjusting each machine so that it works at its greatest efficiency?

5) Woodworking machines create large volumes of waste that, ironically, is not always easy to burn. Can you dispose of this waste?

6) Is working in a dusty atmosphere going to irritate you? This is a problem that is worsened by working in a small workshop. One manufacturer of ventilating equipment tells me that it is not possible to ventilate the workshop to remove the dust, but that if dust is a problem then each machine must have its own ducting in order to reach the minimum air velocity that is required to convey sawdust—a velocity of about 3,000 ft per minute (1,000 m per minute).

7) Machines require space around them so that you can operate them. Do you have the space available in your workshop?

8) Large machines require powerful motors. If a motor is above 1 hp (0.75 kW), it may require its own special wiring into the electrical supply. You will have to find that out from a competent electrician.

Obviously, we are all likely to make use of woodworking machines at some stage despite these powerful arguments. I do think, however, that before you buy a machine for use at home you should consider most carefully the eight points that I have listed.

THE BANDSAW

With a fairly small motor—say ¾ hp (0.563 kW)—the bandsaw can be used for cutting wood up to 6 in (150 mm) thick. It is, therefore, about three times as efficient as a circular saw, and is a safer machine. It can be used to make straight or curved cuts in almost any material, and will cut hardwood, softwood, plywood, blockboard, chipboard, and fibreboard (hardboard) (I even know of someone who uses a bandsaw to cut up the bones for his dogs).

The bandsaw is fairly quiet, is safe, and is a pleasant machine to use. It can make you feel very creative; I would certainly buy a bandsaw before I bought any other machine.

THE INCA BANDSAW (fig. 17)

The Inca bandsaw is made almost entirely of aluminium. It has, therefore, few parts that will rust and is light enough to be moved around the workshop with reasonable ease.

This bandsaw is capable of cutting wood up to 6¼ in (158 mm) thick. The table can be tilted by as much as 45° for angle cutting. The table is fitted with a rip fence to help guide the work when straight-cutting, and the table top is slotted to take a miter guide.

The blade for a bandsaw comes as a continuous loop with the ends brazed together. The blade has to be placed over the wheels, and is tensioned by raising the upper wheel with an allen key—a kind of hexagonal spanner—that is provided with the machine. The upper wheel then has to be tilted by turning a knob on the back of the machine until the

blade runs evenly over both of the wheels. The lower wheel of the Inca bandsaw is turned by an electric motor. My bandsaw is run by a ½-hp (0.375-kW) motor, and I find that that is sufficient power for my needs.

Guides above and below the table prevent the blade from twisting, and lend support to the back of the blade every time that a cut is made. The upper guide can be adjusted vertically, and for the sake of safety and accurate cutting it should be set to just clear the thickness of the work.

Four different widths of woodcutting blades are available for the Inca bandsaw; the narrow blades will cut quicker curves than the wider blades. Many people prefer to fit a metal-cutting blade for woodcutting operations, as they find that a metal-cutting blade will cut a straighter path.

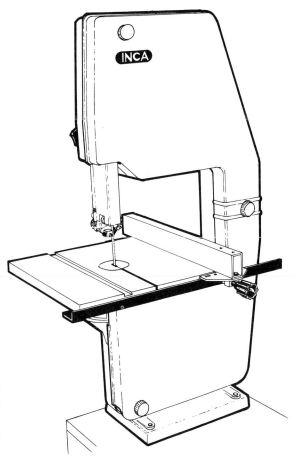

Fig. 17 The Inca bandsaw is made almost entirely of aluminium.

How to fit a new blade on the bandsaw

1) Remove the plug from the electricity supply in order to isolate the motor.

2) Remove the cover from the machine (fig. 18). Take out the plastic insert from the center of the table (fig. 19, A), and remove the fence mechanism.

3) Release the blade guides above and below the table (fig. 19, B, D), and push them well away from the path of the blade.

4) Fit the blade over the wheels and raise the upper wheel, using the adjusting screw until the blade tension indicator reads between 3 and 5 (*see* insert, fig. 18). Wide blades will require a slightly greater tension than narrow blades.

5) Turn the upper wheel by hand in the normal direction for its rotation—take care not to trap your fingers—and simultaneously tilt the wheel by turning the adjusting screw on the back of the machine. Continue to tilt the wheel until the teeth on the blade

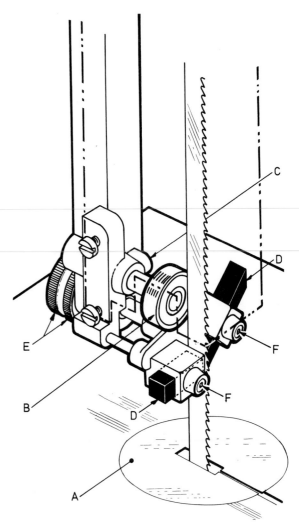

Fig. 19 The working parts on the upper-blade guide of the Inca bandsaw.

protrude slightly from the rubber layer covering both of the wheels. In the case of very narrow blades, the blade teeth must run on the rubber layer that protects the set of the teeth.

6) Push the counter-pressure rollers forward (fig. 19, B) on both guides until the rollers almost touch the back of the blade. Lock the rollers in position by turning the screw provided (fig. 19, C).

7) Bring the blade guide supports (fig. 19, D) forward by turning the nut and locknut (fig. 19, E) until the teeth on the blade are just clear of the guides. Put the blade guide supports (fig. 19, D) lightly against the blade and tighten the screws (fig. 19, F), using the allen key that is provided.

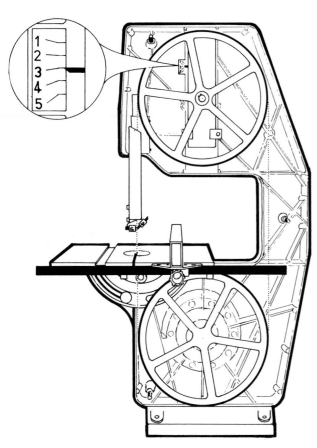

Fig. 18 The cover removed from the Inca bandsaw.

8) Check that you have fitted the blade correctly by rotating the wheels by hand. Then replace the cover and the plastic insert. Switch on the supply.

Care of a bandsaw blade

Occasionally, people have been troubled by blades breaking for no apparent reason. One bandsaw blade manufacturer gives the following hints in order to obtain the maximum life from a blade:

1) Always slacken off the tension screw when the saw is not in use.
2) Do not apply excessive tension to the blade.
3) Keep the guides clean and free running.
4) The blade should only touch the counter-pressure rollers when work is applied to the cutting edge.
5) The teeth of woodcutting blades—not metal-cutting blades—can be resharpened with a triangular file (fig. 20). However, only a bandsaw-type file should be used, as this has rounded corners. Other types of triangular files have sharp corners that induce cracking in the gullets of the teeth.
6) Do not allow the blade to get blunt.

How to use the bandsaw safely

• Lower the upper guide until it just clears the surface of the work.
• Keep your hands well away from the blade. If necessary, use a wooden stick to push your work forward.
• Isolate the machine from the electricity supply before you make any internal adjustments to this machine.
• Make sure the driving belt from the motor to the lower wheel is well-guarded.

Other makes of bandsaws

Other makes of bandsaws to consider for a home workshop are Burgess, DeWalt, Coronet, and Willow. Some of these are three-wheel machines. The third wheel increases the distance between the blade and the frame of the machine so that wide boards can be sawn.

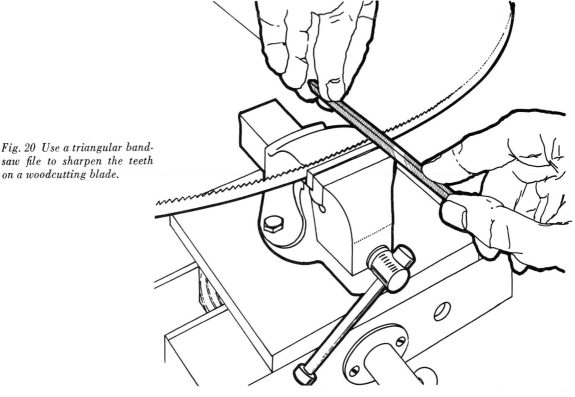

Fig. 20 Use a triangular bandsaw file to sharpen the teeth on a woodcutting blade.

THE RADIAL ARM SAW

The radial arm saw has become popular in the last ten years, so you may be forgiven for thinking that it is a recent invention. In fact, the radial arm saw has been used in industry for over fifty years.

Essentially, this machine tool consists of an electric motor that is suspended from a track on the underside of an arm. The arm is attached to a column at the back of the machine. The arm can be pivoted around the column, and the column can be made to rise and fall. It is possible to make compound adjustments of the motor, which can be swivelled through 360° below the arm and can be turned head-over-heels inside the motor-mounting bracket. A saw blade, or various other attachments, can be fitted to the spindle from the motor so that all work that is placed upon the table can be sawn or shaped at almost any angle. The radial arm saw is, therefore, a versatile machine tool.

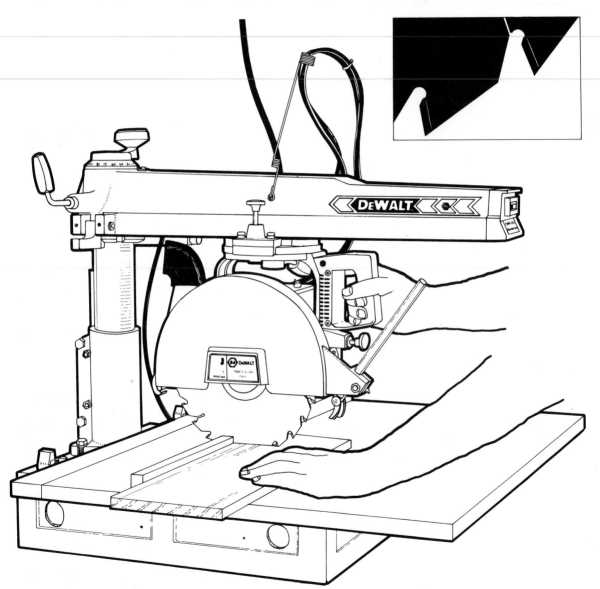

Fig. 21 The DeWalt radial arm saw being used to crosscut. Inset shows part of a tungsten carbide-tipped saw blade with a Teflon^TM (non-stick) coating.

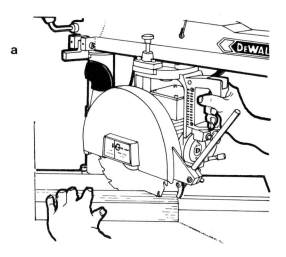

The electric motor on the DeWalt radial arm saw (figs. 21 & 22, b) has a flattened face on the underside; this is the consequence of some advanced design work with electric motors. A flat face on the motor increases the maximum depth of cut. The saw blade is fitted directly onto the motor spindle—there are no gears or belts—so this machine is particularly quiet when free-running. When sawing, however, the machine makes the noise that is typical for any circular saw—this cannot be avoided.

The radial arm saw can crosscut (see fig. 21), miter crosscut (fig. 22, a), and bevel crosscut (fig. 22, b). The crosscut action appears to be very dangerous, but is really no more dangerous than when handsawing, for the work is held against the fence with one hand and the saw is pulled towards the operator with the other hand.

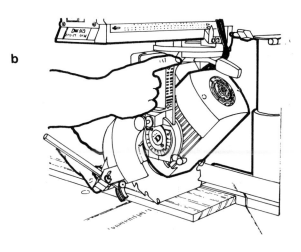

When ripsawing (fig. 22, c), the motor has to be swivelled through 90°, and then locked onto the arm of the machine. The work has to be pushed past the saw blade, so here the action is very different. The hood above the saw blade has to be tilted until the leading edge just clears the work; the claw has to be lowered until the points of the claw are $\frac{1}{8}$ in (3 mm) below the surface of the work; the work has to approach the saw from the correct direction according to the rotation of the saw blade. The purpose of the claw is to catch the work should it bind against the saw blade. Large panels can be easily ripsawed; however, it is difficult ripsawing small pieces.

Fig. 22 The radial arm saw is a versatile machine that can: (a) miter crosscut, (b) bevel crosscut, (c) ripsaw.

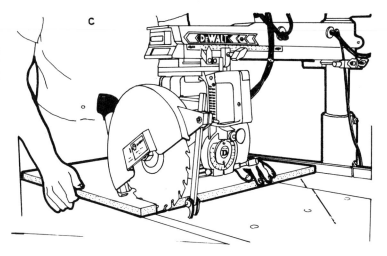

The table of the DeWalt radial arm saw has been made of chipboard. You will find that the blade cuts a shallow path in the table—this cannot be avoided. I have heard of some people covering the entire surface of the table with a sheet of fibreboard (hardboard), which can eventually be discarded for a new piece.

The radial arm saw must be set up carefully if it is to be used accurately. There are a number of adjustments that have to be made, and you must read the booklet supplied with the machine to find out about these. Once set up, the machine will remain accurate for a long period of time.

How to fit a new blade to the radial arm saw

Tungsten carbide-tipped saw blades are worth the extra cost since they cut more cleanly than ordinary blades and stay sharp longer. When ordering a new blade, specify the outside diameter of the blade, the diameter of the spindle, the speed of rotation of the spindle, and say that it is required for a radial arm saw.

To fit a new blade:
1) Remove the plug from the electricity supply in order to isolate the motor.
2) Follow the instructions supplied with your machine. Usually this means: a) holding the spindle stationary by placing the allen key provided into the end of the spindle, b) removing the large nut from the end of the spindle using a spanner—note that it may be a left-hand thread, c) removing the washer and the old blade, noting the direction of the teeth on the old blade, d) fitting the new blade and reassembling the parts in reverse order, and e) tightening the large nut securely.

How to use the radial arm saw safely

- Read the instruction manual.
- Check that all clamp handles are tight.
- If crosscutting:
1) Position the work on the table.
2) Switch on the motor while it is positioned at the back of the table.
3) With one hand hold the work against the fence, and with the other hand pull the motor steadily towards yourself.
4) Return the motor to its position at the back of the table.

5) Switch off the motor and wait for the blade to stop rotating before you remove your work from the table.
- If ripsawing:
1) Prepare to feed the work from the correct side of the table, taking into account the direction of rotation of the blade.
2) Tilt the hood above the saw until the leading edge on the hood just clears the thickness of the work.
3) Lower the claw until the points on the claw are approximately 1/8 in (3 mm) below the surface of the work.
4) Switch on the motor.
5) Use a wooden stick to push small pieces of wood past the saw blade.
6) Switch off the motor and wait for the blade to stop rotating.
7) Do not attempt to ripsaw pieces of wood shorter than 12 in (300 mm).
- Keep the saw blade sharp.
- Periodically check and align the parts as advised in the instruction manual.

Other makes of radial arm saws

Other makes of radial arm saws to consider are Susemill and Shopmate.

THE MACHINE PLANER

The machine planer helps you to prepare wood from a rough state to a smooth finish. In addition to planing, it can also make rabbets, chamfers, and tapered shapes. The machine planer works on a different principle from hand-planing; when hand-planing, the blade remains fixed in the body of the plane, but when machine-planing there are at least two blades that revolve with a steel cylindrical block. A table on either side of the cylindrical block helps you to remove a controlled amount of waste from your wood. The back table has to be set level with the cutting edges of the blades; the front table has to be adjusted for the thickness of cut that you require.

The machine planer should remove a 1/8-in (3-mm) thickness of cut at one time. If you remove less wood than this, then the blades tend to rub against the work and become dull quite quickly. If you remove more wood than the $\frac{1}{8}$-in (3-mm) thickness the motor will labor unnecessarily. A machine planer is a noisy machine, and you will find its use is made more comfortable when you wear ear protectors. On its own, the machine planer is not a very useful machine in the home workshop; however, if it is fitted with a thicknessing attachment you can get good use out of it.

THE CORONET MACHINE PLANER AND THICKNESSER

The coronet machine planer (fig. 23, a) will plane wood up to $4\frac{1}{2}$ in (115 mm) wide and of any length. I have found that it works satisfactorily from a $\frac{1}{2}$-hp (0.375-kW) electric motor running at 3,000 rpm. The cylindrical block is belt-driven from the motor. The pulleys must be chosen so that the cylindrical block runs at a speed between 4,000 and 6,000 rpm.

The back table on this machine is permanently set at the same height as the cutting edges on the blades. The front table is adjustable in height and must be set to about $\frac{1}{8}$ in (3 mm) below the level of the back table.

The machine planer is used to produce a smooth finish on one side of the work. The work is then machine-planed again, with the smooth side against the fence of the machine; this produces a smooth edge which is at right angles to the smooth side. These two planed surfaces are commonly called the face-side and the face-edge.

The two remaining rough surfaces are then planed parallel to the smooth surfaces with the thicknessing attachment (fig. 23, b). Two steel springs on this attachment press a smooth surface on the work upwards onto the thicknessing table. This thicknessing table is adjustable in height so that the work can be finished at any preset thickness from 4 in (100 mm) to $\frac{1}{25}$ in (1 mm). Clearly, the wood must be planed in stages, with no more than about $\frac{1}{8}$-in (3-mm) thickness of waste being removed at one time.

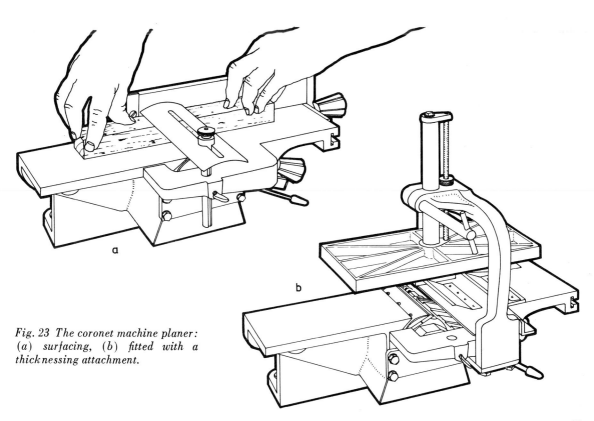

Fig. 23 The coronet machine planer: (a) surfacing, (b) fitted with a thicknessing attachment.

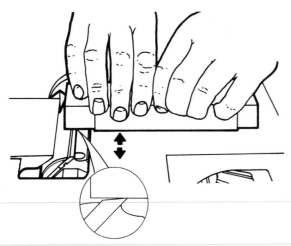

Fig. 24 Sharpening the blades of a machine planer: Notice the cylindrical block is wedged to stop it rotating, and the oilstone is partially rested on one of the tables.

Sharpening the blades

Sharpening the blades is a task that occurs fairly frequently, so it is something that you must be able to tackle for yourself.

1) Remove the plug from the electricity supply in order to isolate the motor.

2) Lower the front table by about $\frac{1}{8}$ in (3 mr below the level of the back table.

3) Fix the cylindrical block with a wooden wedge so that the block cannot revolve, but before that, turn the block so that when your oilstone is resting on the front table the oilstone is also resting across the bevel of the blade (fig. 24). Wrap part of the oilstone in a sheet of paper so the oilstone does not touch the front table.

4) Apply some light machine oil to the blade, and rub the oilstone along the blade several times. Revolve the cylindrical block so that you can sharpen the other blade. Make sure the bevels on both the blades are the same size.

5) After many sharpenings, the blades will have to be returned to the manufacturer or a machine-tool sharpening firm in your area to be ground and balanced. To avoid delay, keep a spare set of blades for your machine planer.

Fitting new blades

1) Remove the plug from the electricity supply in order to isolate the motor.

2) The blades are usually fixed into the cylindrical block with allen screws. Slacken these screws and remove the blades.

3) Insert the new blades the same way around as the old ones, and gently tighten the end allen screws until these screws lightly grip the blades.

4) The blades must project from the cylindrical block by a very short distance. This distance can be determined by placing a length of planed wood on the back table. When the cylindrical block is revolved by hand each cutter should carry the piece of wood forward by $\frac{1}{8}$ in (3 mm). The blades must be adjusted so that they cut evenly along their length. Usually, there are adjusting screws on the cylindrical block that enable you to make these fine adjustments.

5) Fully tighten all the allen screws so that each blade is held firmly. Check that the setting of each blade has not been disturbed.

How to use the machine planer safely

- Keep the blades sharp.
- Make sure that the belt drive is well-guarded.
- Do not attempt to machine-plane pieces of wood of less than 12 in (300 mm) in length.
- Wear ear protectors, as the noise can cause you to make irrational judgments.
- If surface-planing:

1) Set the guard over the cylindrical block so that your work just passes underneath the guard.

2) Check each piece of wood to see that the grain direction will not cause digging in. If necessary, you must turn the wood around.

3) If the wood is warped, then the hollow side should be the first side to be planed (fig. 25).

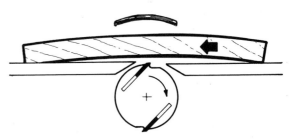

Fig. 25 When wood is warped, the hollow side should be the first to be machine-planed.

4) Press the wood firmly onto the front table, and push the wood slowly under the guard. Press down onto the wood as it reappears on the back table.

• Do not feed the wood too quickly, as the cuts made by the blades can become noticeable as a series of ridges. In any case, the work should be planed again lightly by hand before polishing.

Other makes of machine planers

Other makes of machine planers to consider are the Myford and the Inca.

THE ELECTRIC DRILL

As the electric drill has been developed it has become safer, more powerful, and more compact.

Today, most electric drills are of double-insulated construction. If a drill is double-insulated, then it will have the international symbol ▣ marked on the body of the drill. A double-insulated drill will only have a two-core cord; there is no grounding (earth lead). The safety of the drill is derived from two electrical barriers that are, in addition to the normal insulation, given to the motor. The manufacturer usually provides these barriers by bonding a sleeve of insulating material to the armature of the motor, and by making the body around the motor of a non-conducting material. If a fault occurs inside a double-insulated electric drill you will be perfectly safe, but you must take care not to get the drill wet and not to drill into a live cable.

There are some all-insulated drills available. These are even safer than a double-insulated drill. On an all-insulated drill the gearbox and the chuck spindle are made of a non-conducting material, so there is no metal part on the outside of the drill that has contact with a metal part inside the drill.

If you intend using the drill mainly out-of-doors or near water you should consider buying a low-voltage drill that operates through a transformer. Clearly, in addition to buying the drill you also have to buy a transformer.

The power of a drill is shown on the body of the drill. This number is usually expressed as the watts input. If a drill is to perform its task properly, then it must be of at least 300 watts input.

As electric motors have become more powerful, manufacturers have been able to fit larger chucks to the drills. Most electric drills are now fitted with chucks that can hold work up to $\frac{1}{2}$ in (13 mm) in diameter.

A drill is made more versatile when it contains a speed-changing device. If you are drilling small holes, you require a faster speed than if you are drilling large holes. One type of speed-changing device is electronic, but a better type is a manual gearbox, for when the manual gearbox is used to reduce the chuck speed the torque at the chuck is increased. Two-speed drills and four-speed drills are obtainable, but as my tool supplier said, "The simpler the drill, the less to go wrong."

STANLEY BRIDGES ELECTRIC DRILL 1023

The Stanley Bridges electric drill is a double-insulated electric drill (fig. 26). One turn of a knob on the side of the gearbox provides speeds of 2,850 or 1,075 rpm. The chuck can have a diameter as big as $\frac{1}{2}$ in (12 mm). The motor is rated at 400 watts input under no load conditions, and is capable of drilling holes with diameters of up to $1\frac{1}{4}$ in (32 mm) in wood.

Some accessories can be used with electric drills, and the bench stand is one of the most useful of these (see fig. 26). It is a good idea to bolt the bench stand onto a piece of blockboard; then the stand can be quickly fastened to the bench with the bench dogs or C clamps (G cramps).

When drilling wood you will require a set of high-speed steel drills within the size range $\frac{1}{16}$ in–$\frac{1}{4}$ in (1.5 mm–6 mm) (see fig. 3, h). These drills become expensive above the $\frac{1}{4}$-in (6-mm) size; a cheaper drill for larger holes is called a spade bit.

How to use the electric drill safely

• Switch off the power before changing attachments.
• Tighten the chuck fully by turning the chuck key in all three holes around the chuck.
• Remove the chuck key from the chuck.
• Do not get the drill wet.
• Take care not to drill into live electric cables.

Other makes of electric drills

Other makes of electric drills to consider are Black & Decker, Bosch, Rockwell, Shopmate, and Wolf. Wolf has manufactured electric drills that are all-insulated.

A plea from the author

Could a manufacturer please produce a silent electric drill?

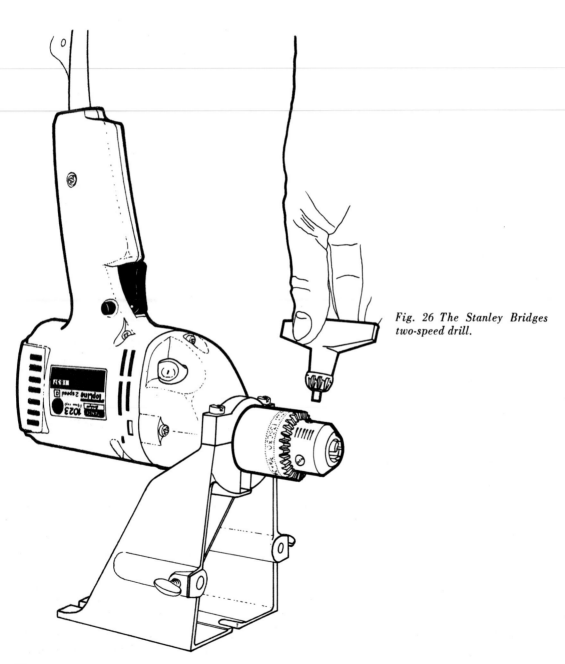

Fig. 26 The Stanley Bridges two-speed drill.

THE MORTISING MACHINE

The mortising machine will rapidly and accurately cut mortises—rectangular slots—in any hardwood or softwood. The principle on which the machine works is for a drill to rotate inside a hollow square chisel. The drill bores a round hole in the work and the chisel shapes the hole into a square. A mortise is created by making a series of cuts alongside each other.

In practice, the mortise should be cut in easy stages until full depth has been reached. This is because the chisel tends to jam in the work when a single hole is cut to a great depth. There is a device on the machine that prevents the work from lifting with the chisel after each cut. There are also guides on the machine that enable woodworkers to accurately position their work below the chisel. These guides help you to produce accurate mortises with minimal marking-out.

The small mortising machines are powered by an electric drill, so they tend to be noisy. You will find that they are more comfortable to operate if you wear ear protectors.

THE A & T MORTISING MACHINE

The A & T mortising machine (fig. 27) is powered by an electric drill. A series of different-sized collars is provided with this machine so that almost any make of electric drill can be fitted. The drill can be raised and lowered by a lever with a maximum movement of $2\frac{7}{8}$ in (73 mm). This amount of movement can be accurately reduced by turning a depth-stop screw.

Chisels and bits in the sizes of $\frac{1}{4}$ in (6 mm), $\frac{3}{8}$ in (9 mm), and $\frac{1}{2}$ in (12 mm) are available to fit this machine. These are expensive, but you do not have to buy the complete size range. If you are interested in furniture construction, then the $\frac{1}{4}$-in (6-mm) chisel-and-bit combination is all that you require.

How to fit a new chisel and bit

Here is a method that ensures there is a $\frac{1}{16}$-in (2-mm) clearance between the cutting edges on the chisel and the cutting edges on the bit.

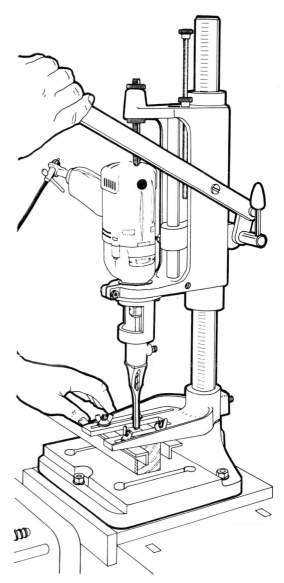

Fig. 27 The A & T mortising machine can be powered by almost any electric drill.

1) Select the chisel-and-bit combination of a size that suits your work.

2) Slide the chisel into the holder beneath the chuck of the drill, but allow a space of the thickness of a coin between the shoulder of the chisel and the face of the holder. Temporarily lock the chisel into position and slide the bit fully up through the hol-

low chisel. Securely lock the bit into the chuck on the drill, using the chuck key.

3) Release the locking screw on the chisel and push the chisel fully home. Retighten the locking screw, making sure that the chisel is right on the work.

Sharpening the chisel

After a few hours' use, the chisel should be removed from the holder so that the cutting edges on the chisel can be sharpened. Sharpening is carried out by turning a sharpening tool of the correct size inside the cutting edges on the chisel. All that is required are a few turns of the sharpening bit by hand (fig. 28).

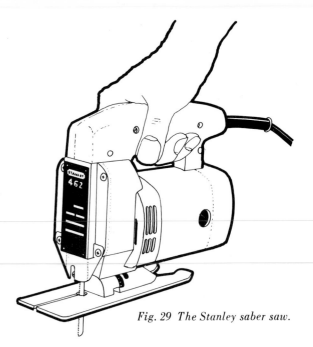

Fig. 29 The Stanley saber saw.

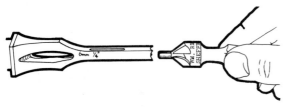

Fig. 28 The special sharpening tool sharpens the cutting edges on a machine mortise chisel.

How to use the mortising machine safely

The hollow, square-chisel mortising machine is a safe machine provided that you operate it with reasonable care.

Other makes of mortising machines

Another make of mortising machine that you could consider for the home workshop is the Wolf.

THE SABER SAW

The saber saw is a portable electric tool that can be moved to the woodworker's work. The work needs to be clamped or held on the bench with sufficient space below the marked line for the blade to pass. The blade reciprocates and is capable of cutting straight or curved paths. By using different blades, this saw can also be used to cut wood, thermoplastics, aluminium, or mild steel.

THE STANLEY SABER SAW, TYPE 462

The Stanley saber saw, type 462 (fig. 29), is a double-insulated saw. It is capable of cutting wood up to 1 in (25 mm) thick. The sole plate can be tilted so that the machine can saw on an angle of up to 30° to the right, and up to 45° to the left. A graduated scale is provided on the tool to indicate the angle of the cut.

The sole plate is curved upwards along its front edge so that the machine can be tilted forward to make a pocket cut (plunge cut) in the center of the work. In addition to pocket-cutting, the sole plate can be turned through 180° so that plastic and laminated sheets can be cut with very little chipping of the edges of the cut. Since the saw cuts on the up-stroke, it is better to do all the marking-out on the back of your material. Any slight chipping along the edges of the cut will then be on the back of your work.

How to fit a new blade

Fitting a new blade is usually quite simple, but do read the instructions supplied with the machine. Usually fitting consists of slackening off the blade-retaining screw, pulling out the blade, pushing in a new blade, and tightening the retaining screw.

How to use the saber saw safely

• Keep the cord well away from the marked line that you are following. If possible, drape the cord over your shoulder.
• Make sure that the trailing cord is not a hazard to other people.

Other makes of saber saws

Other makes of saber saws to consider are Black & Decker, Bosch, Rockwell, and Shopmate.

THE BELT SANDER

The belt sander is a portable electric tool that is moved to the work. It is used to prepare large surfaces to a state that is ready for polishing. The abrasive belt can be changed easily, so if the surface is very rough it is better to initially use a belt with a coarse abrasive, and to work down in stages to finish with a belt with a fine abrasive. The type of abrasive that is used on these belts is usually aluminium oxide. It is important that a new belt is fitted the correct way around; otherwise, the join in the belt may be forced apart by the sanding action. It is equally important that you do not apply excessive pressure when using the machine, as this will cause overloading and can result in premature deterioration of the motor.

THE STANLEY BELT SANDER, TYPE 497

The Stanley belt sander (fig. 30) is a two-speed machine. It comes fitted with an abrasive belt that is 4 in (100 mm) wide, but you can use the belt sander to sand as large an area as you wish. A vacuum bag collects the sanding dust from the abrasive belt. This bag should be emptied when it is about quarter-full.

The abrasive belt is tracked with a simple adjusting screw, and is correctly positioned when it runs flush with the outer end of the rear drive pulley.

How to change abrasive belts

Disconnect the machine from the power supply. Hold the machine by the two handles, and stand it

on the front pulley with the belt vertical. Push downwards until the front pulley is retracted and is locked automatically.

Replace the sanding belt, making sure that the arrows on the belt are in the same direction as the arrows on the data plate on the side of the machine.

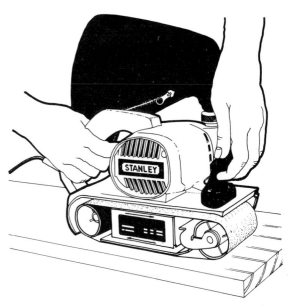

Fig. 30 The Stanley belt sander is a two-speed machine.

To release the front pulley, rest the heel of your right hand on the front of the plate. Extend your fingers around and up and over the front pulley, and pull down.

How to use the belt sander safely

Read the operating instructions in the manual.
The procedure usually is as follows:
1) Secure your work to the bench.
2) Take a firm grasp of both handles.
3) Raise the machine above your work and switch on.
4) When the motor has gathered speed, lower the machine gently onto your work.
5) Do not press downwards, but allow the natural weight of the machine to apply pressure for you.
6) Traverse the machine over the surface of your work.

7) Avoid tilting the machine, as the edge of the belt can make a gash in your work.

8) Raise the machine above your work, and switch off.

9) Wait for the belt to stop moving before you put the machine down.

A sensible place to put the machine so that it cannot be knocked over is on the floor. Make sure that the trailing cord is not a hazard to other people.

Keep the cord well away from your work.

Read the maintenance instructions in the manual; they will tell you about clearing dust from inside the machine, greasing the machine, and inspecting the carbon brushes.

Other makes of belt sanders

Other makes of belt sanders to consider are Rockwell, and Wolf.

ELECTRIC MOTORS

If you buy an electric motor for a woodworking machine, ask for one that is of the fan-cooled, totally enclosed type, with a capacitor starter. Electric motors not of the totally enclosed type that are fitted to woodworking machines suffer badly from the dust that is drawn through them. Note that the starting current for an electric motor is likely to be higher than the running current, so you will be unable to fit the largest motor that your electricity supply appears able to bear. However, motors of ½ hp (0.375 kW), which are adequate for the small machines I have described in this book, can usually be plugged into the ordinary domestic supply.

A motor with a speed of about 1,500 rpm is a good choice for a slow-running machine like a bandsaw. A faster running machine such as a machine planer is better operated by a motor running at about 3,000 rpm.

Every motor should be wired through its own starter switch. Ideally, this switch should be operated by push-buttons. The switch should be fitted with first, a thermal overload that will trip the switch if you happen to overload the motor, and second, a no-volt release device, which is a safety device that will trip the switch if the electricity supply happens

to fail. In either event, the motor is restarted by pushing the starter button. If you are going to complete the wiring-in of a starter motor you should ask for clear wiring instructions from your machine tool supplier. The task is not difficult, but it is a little complex.

MAKING A STAND FOR A MACHINE TOOL

A strong stand can be made for a machine tool using 3-in (75-mm) × 2-in (50-mm) ready-dressed (planed) softwood, and 1-in (25-mm) thick blockboard (fig. 31). As the illustration shows, the lower rails can be fastened to the legs with coach bolts, and the upper rails fastened to the legs with rabbet joints that are glued and screwed. The remaining parts can be glued and screwed together.

A stand needs to be sufficiently long and deep for it to be stable. This usually means making the stand at least 16 in (400 mm) long × 16 in (400 mm) deep. Positioning the motor low has the effect of increasing the stability. The height of the stand should position the machine at a height that is comfortable for the operator. The stands I have made have usually finished about 25 in (640 mm) high.

The machine has to be bolted through the blockboard top of the stand. Provision has to be made in the top for the belt drive from the motor. Remember that the belt drive should be well guarded so that the belt cannot be touched while the machine is in operation. Provision also has to be made for the waste to fall easily, yet tidily, from the machine.

TOOL CARE

Rust is a problem that I have not yet mentioned. Tools that are kept in a garden workshop frequently rust. Oddly, I find that rusting is less of a problem in the winter than it is in the spring, probably because exposed metal surfaces suffer more from condensation in the spring. The answer is to keep tools in boxes or to spray all steel surfaces with a spray such as Lubysil 717. There are other sprays available, but I have found this one to be the best—although not the most easily obtainable. Lubysil 717 comes in a handy aerosol can, and a quick spray gives the surfaces a transparent and imperceptible coating that remains effective for a very long time.

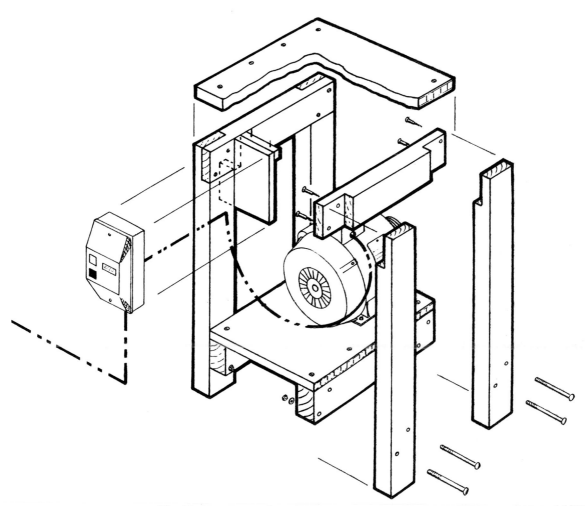

Fig. 31 A strong stand can be made for a machine tool.

REDWOOD
WHITEWOOD

TEAK

CHESTNUT

REDWOOD
WHITEWOOD

MAHOGANY

AFRORMOSIA
AGBA
IROKO
MAHOGANY
MAKORE
MANSONIA
UTILE
WALNUT

EUCALYPTUS
MAPLE
WALNUT

0°
30°
30°
60°
60°
120°
60°
30°
30°
0°

△ softwoods

○ hardwoods

Fig. 32 A world map showing the main softwood and hardwood growing areas and the names of some of the most frequently used species.

Woods

There are over seventy species of softwoods and three hundred and forty species of hardwoods in fairly common use today. A world map (fig. 32) shows the main softwood and hardwood growing areas, and names some of the most frequently used species. A fuller list of species is given in Appendix B.

The words "softwoods" and "hardwoods" are misnomers, for the main difference between the two groups is not that the softwoods are necessarily soft and the hardwoods hard, but that the softwoods are usually evergreens and the hardwoods are usually deciduous. The softwoods are commonly used for painted work and for structural work, whereas the hardwoods are usually used for furniture making.

When buying wood you should ask for it to be dressed (machine planed) to the sizes given in the cutting list. The extra cost of machine planing is small compared to the work planing the wood down to size would entail. In addition, when the wood has been dressed you can check more carefully the quality of what you are buying.

Make sure the wood has no splits, and that it is dry. The drying of wood is called "seasoning"; you can ask your lumber dealer if the wood has been well-seasoned. The wood should have a moisture content of below 20 percent. You will have to take the word of your lumber dealer for the state of the seasoning, but if later you find that your wood shrinks drastically you should avoid buying from that source again. Even if you get satisfaction from one source it pays to swap allegiances, because the market is constantly changing. I recently bought a quantity of wood from one lumber dealer, only to find out later that I could have bought the same quantity of wood from another dealer for one-fifth of the price.

To find your nearest lumber retailer look through the Yellow Pages and the pages of your local newspaper. You may find that hardwoods and softwoods are sold by separate retailers, and that manufactured boards such as plywood, fibreboard (hardboard), and chipboard are sold by a third type of retailer. Before placing a large order, such as the wood for a sideboard, ask for a quotation.

SOME FREQUENTLY USED SPECIES

SOFTWOODS

1) Redwood or Scots Pine or Red Deal
(Russia, Baltic, Canada)
Pinus sylvestris
This is a reddish to yellowish-brown softwood.
2) Whitewood or European Spruce
(Russia, Baltic, Canada)
Picea abies
This is a light yellowish-brown softwood. It has a mildly lustrous surface when planed.

HARDWOODS

1) Afrormosia or Kokrodua (W. Africa)
Afrormosia elata
This is a brownish-yellow wood with darker streaks. It is very stable and is sometimes regarded as a substitute for teak; however, it has a finer texture than teak and it does not have an oily nature.
2) Agba or Tola (W. Africa)
Cossweilerodendron balsamiferum
This wood is a pale yellow straw color. It is straight-grained, has a fairly close, even texture, and works well. It has a distinctive mild peppery smell.
3) Sweet Chestnut or Spanish Chestnut (Europe)
Castanea sativa
Chestnut is yellow-brown and resembles English oak, but it is softer than oak and is much easier to work.

4) Eucalyptus or Mountain Ash or Tasmanian Oak (Australia and Tasmania)

Eucalyptus regnans

This wood is light brown, but darkens with exposure. It is straight-grained, moderately hard, and fairly easy to work. It has no characteristic taste or smell.

5) Iroko (W. Africa)

Chlorophora excelsa

Iroko as bark is yellow, but turns a golden brown with exposure to light. It is a useful wood as it can be used indoors and outdoors. It is sometimes used as a substitute for teak.

6) Honduras Mahogany or Cuban Mahogany (Central and S. America)

Swietenia macrophylia

This is a yellow to deep rich brown. It is a very stable wood and is easily worked. It finishes well and can be used both indoors and outdoors.

7) Sapele Mahogany (W. Africa)

Entandrophragma cylindricum

This wood is found near the town of Sapele in West Africa. It is a red wood with a pronounced stripe, making it awkward to plane. It is one of the harder mahoganies and is not suitable for use by a beginner.

8) Makore or Cherry Mahogany (W. Africa)

Mimusops heckelii

This is reddish brown with dark streaks. The wood is neither a true cherry nor a true mahogany. It is heavier than mahogany and of a finer texture. The dust from this wood can irritate.

9) Mansonia (W. Africa)

Mansonia altissima

Mansonia is purple-brown. It is a fairly hard wood, usually with a straight grain and smooth texture. It is sometimes used as a substitute for walnut. The dust can be very irritating when sanding.

10) Queensland Maple or Silk Wood (Australia)

Flindersia brayleyana

This wood is pinkish brown, darkening to medium brown. It has a mild pleasant smell. It has an interlocked or wavy grain that is sometimes marked with ripples. It polishes well.

11) Teak (Burma, India, Thailand)

Tectona grandis

Teak varies from golden to chocolate brown. This wood is strong and durable and can be used indoors and outdoors. It has a greasy nature that can make it difficult to glue.

12) Utile (W. Africa)

Entandrophragma utile

This is red mahogany. It is a popular hardwood and is easily obtained. Utile is closely related to sapele mahogany, but it is more stable and easier to work.

13) African Walnut or Lovoawood or Nigerian Golden Walnut or Tigerwood (W. Africa)

Lova klaineana

This wood is golden brown with thin black streaks. It is not a true walnut, but it is sometimes used as a substitute. It has a handsome stripey grain, but is unsuitable for use by beginners.

14) Australian Walnut or Australian Laurel or Queensland Walnut (Australia)

Endiandra palmerstonii

This is a dark brown wood with greyish green stripes. It has a slightly lustrous surface when planed. This wood can be difficult to saw.

Cutting Joints by Hand

Learning to cut joints by hand is important, for many woodworkers either dislike using machine tools or just don't have the tools available. Of course, hand work is slower than machine work, but it is quieter—and achieving the skills using hand tools can in itself be rewarding. Woodworkers who have machines can always find ways of reproducing joints like these.

Let's assume that all the joints have been fully marked out. Remember that a marking knife—and sometimes a gauge—is the tool used to mark lines that have to be accurately followed by a saw, whereas a pencil is used merely for marking guidelines on the wood and for cross-hatching waste areas.

DOWEL JOINT

The dowel joint (fig. 33, a) can be used instead of almost any joint. It is the simplest of all joints and is commonly used in the mass production of furniture. It makes the construction of our work easy, but there are some people who say that the dowel joint is not the joint of a craftsman.

MAKING THE DOWEL JOINT

The greatest problem in successfully making a dowel joint is that of accurately aligning the parts (fig. 33, b). I solve this problem by partially inserting two small nails into one half of the joint, nipping the heads off the nails with pincers, then pushing both parts of the joint together. The nails mark the dowel positions, but of course you must pull out the nails before you drill the holes for the dowels.

The depth for the holes can be marked on the drill bit with colored tape—you can use either masking tape or first-aid tape. Drill the holes usually to a depth of 1 in (25 mm).

The dowels can be glued and inserted with a hammer immediately, but I prefer to cut a glue-escape groove along the dowel using a saw (fig. 34). Clamps help to keep the joint together until the glue has set.

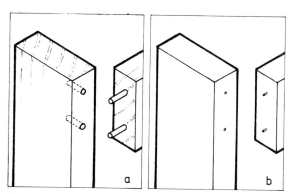

Fig. 33 The dowel joint: (a) completed, (b) marked-out.

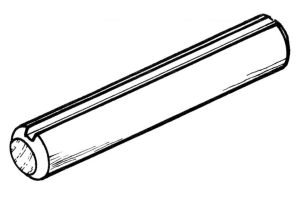

Fig. 34 Use a backsaw to cut a glue-escape groove along a dowel.

END RABBET JOINT

The end rabbet joint (lap butt joint), (fig. 35, a), can be used on boxes. This is a better joint than a plain rabbet joint (plain butt joint) because the end rabbet joint creates a larger gluing surface and helps woodworkers locate the parts accurately. The joint usually penetrates one-third the thickness of the wood. Check that you have done the marking-out correctly (fig. 35, b).

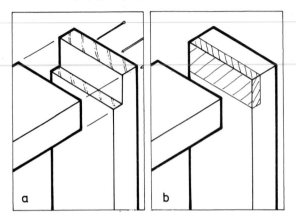

Fig. 35 The end rabbet joint: (a) completed, (b) marked-out.

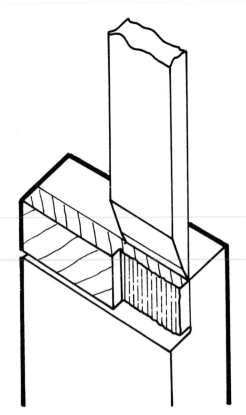

Fig. 37 Clear away the waste with a mallet and a wide firmer chisel.

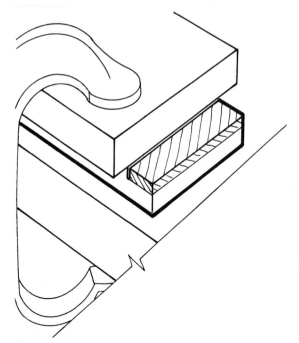

Fig. 36 C-clamp a square-edged block of wood across your work, and use this as a guide for the backsaw.

CUTTING THE JOINT

C-clamp a square-edged block of wood across your work, and use this as a guide for the back-saw (fig. 36). Saw down on the waste side of the rabbet line as far as the marking gauge line.

Next, stand your work upright in the vise and clear (cleave) away the waste with a mallet and a wide firmer chisel (fig. 37). This method works well on softwoods, which are straight-grained, but some hardwoods have an interlocking grain; then the waste is easier to remove with the rabbet plane.

MORTISE-AND-TENON JOINT

The mortise-and-tenon joint (fig. 38, a) can be used on tables, chairs, stools, and doors. Check that you have marked out the joint correctly (fig. 38, b).

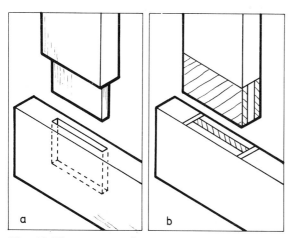

Fig. 38 The mortise-and-tenon joint: (a) completed, (b) marked-out.

CHOPPING THE MORTISE

C-clamp the wood containing the mortise to the top of the bench. Do not forget to place a piece of scrap wood between the shoe on the clamp and the surface of your work to prevent the shoe from making an imprint. It is also advisable to clamp your wood at a place on the bench where the bench top is well supported by a leg of the bench; this will reduce the amount of vibration.

Hit the mortise chisel twice quite firmly with the mallet. Move the chisel a short distance along the mortise and repeat the blows (fig. 39). You can place a piece of colored sticky tape around the blade of the chisel to mark the depth of penetration that is required. You may have to chop over the mortise several times before full depth is reached. The waste can be removed from inside the mortise with a smaller chisel or the small blade of a penknife, but make sure you don't round over the corners of the joint.

CUTTING THE TENON

Place the wood for the tenon on a slope in the vise. Use a backsaw to cut down on the waste side of the line as far as the first diagonal (fig. 40).

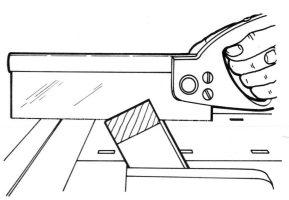

Fig. 40 Use a backsaw to cut down on the waste side of the line as far as the first diagonal.

It is important to cut on the waste side of the line, as this ensures that the tenon will be a good fit in the mortise. Turn the wood over and saw down to the second diagonal. Then hold the wood upright in the vise and saw down to the rabbet line of the joint.

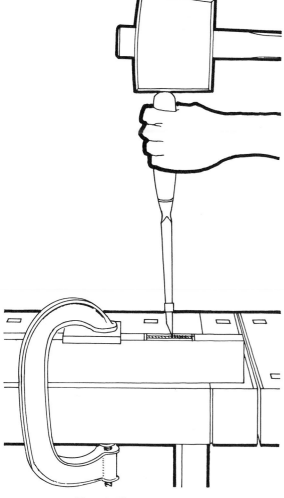

Fig. 39 Chopping the mortise.

The side pieces—called "cheeks"—are removed by holding the wood on a bench hook and carefully sawing on the waste side of the rabbet line with a backsaw (fig. 41).

A ⅛-in (3-mm) cover on each side of the tenon has to be marked out in pencil and cut with a backsaw. These covers help to conceal the ends of the mortise.

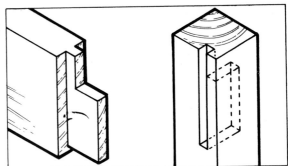

Fig. 42 The square haunched mortise-and-tenon joint.

with the front part of the backsaw (fig. 43). Pare away the waste between the two saw cuts using a mortise chisel.

You can see from the illustration (fig. 43) that some waste wood remains on the end of the work. This helps to prevent the work from splitting while you chop the mortise. The waste can remain intact until the joint has been glued together; then it can be removed with a backsaw.

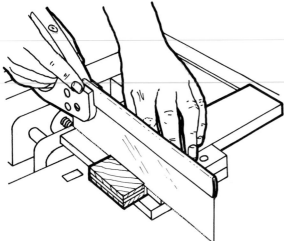

Fig. 41 Remove the side pieces by carefully sawing on the waste side of the rabbet line.

SQUARE HAUNCHED MORTISE-AND-TENON JOINT

The square haunched mortise-and-tenon joint (fig. 42) is often used between the leg and the rail on a table, and is also used to make the corner of a door. The haunch—the small part of the joint—is square on the end, and in the other direction it occupies about one-third the width of the rail.

CHOPPING THE MORTISE

Chop the mortise in the usual way. If you are unsure about how this is done see the mortise-and-tenon joint (fig. 39).

Remove the square haunch by sawing down the sides of the mortise to a depth of ½ in (6 mm)

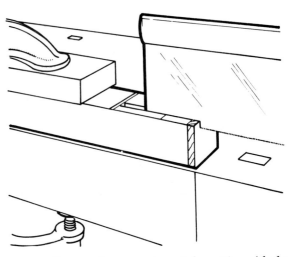

Fig. 43 Remove the square haunch by cutting with the front part of the backsaw, then chiselling out the waste.

CUTTING THE TENON

Cut the tenon in the usual way (see figs. 40 & 41). Use a pencil to mark the haunch and the ⅛-in (3-mm) cover on the tenon. Remove both of these parts with a backsaw. The tenon can then be fitted into the mortise.

SECRET HAUNCHED MORTISE-AND-TENON JOINT

The secret haunched mortise-and-tenon joint (fig. 44) is frequently used between the leg and the rail on a stool. It is a situation in which the square haunch would show, so the haunch has to be sloped in order to conceal itself. The secret haunch occupies about one-third the width of the rail.

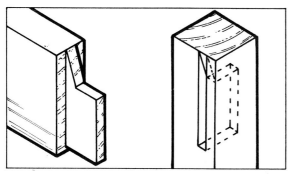

Fig. 44 The secret haunched mortise-and-tenon joint.

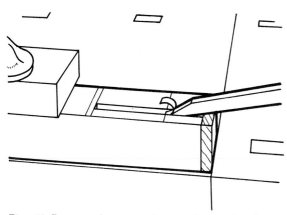

Fig. 45 Remove the secret haunch by cutting on an angle with the front part of the backsaw, then chiselling out the waste on an angle.

CHOPPING THE MORTISE

Chop the mortise in the usual way. If you are unsure about how this is done see the mortise-and-tenon joint (fig. 39).

Remove the secret haunch by sawing down the sides of the mortise on a slope with the front part

of the backsaw. This has to be sawn to a depth of ¼ in (6 mm) inside the mortise. Pare away the waste between the two saw cuts with a mortise chisel (fig. 45).

CUTTING THE TENON

Cut the tenon in the usual way (*see* figs. 40 & 41). Use a pencil to mark the secret haunch and the ⅛-in (3-mm) cover on the tenon. Remove both of these parts using a backsaw. The tenon can then be fitted into the mortise.

MORTISE-AND-TENON WITH DADO

The mortise-and-tenon with dado (fig. 46, a) can be used for the upright division of a cabinet. Check that you have marked out the dado correctly (fig. 46, b).

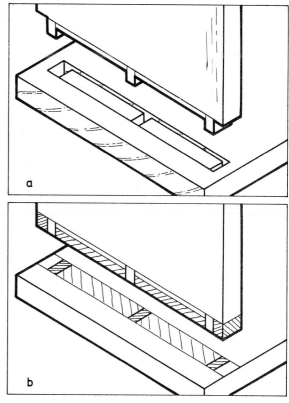

Fig. 46 The mortise-and-tenon with dado: (a) completed, (b) marked-out.

CHOPPING THE MORTISES AND THE DADOS

Chop the mortises in the usual way to a depth of about two-thirds the thickness of the wood. If you are unsure about how this is done see the mortise-and-tenon joint (fig. 39).

Using a wide firmer chisel and a mallet, chop the dados to a depth of $\frac{1}{8}$ in (3 mm) (fig. 47). Sticky tape around the blade of the chisel will mark the depth of penetration that you require.

Use a router to level the bottom of the dado to a depth of $\frac{1}{8}$ in (3 mm) (fig. 48).

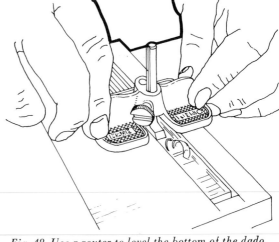

Fig. 48 Use a router to level the bottom of the dado.

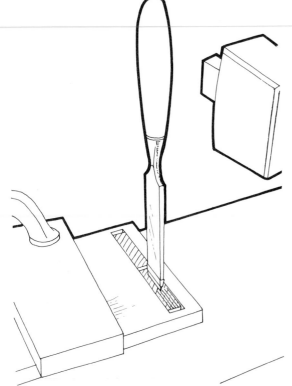

Fig. 47 Chop the dado to a depth of $\frac{1}{8}$ in (3 mm) with a wide firmer chisel and a mallet.

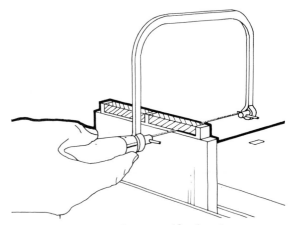

Fig. 49 Saw down on the waste side of each tenon.

CUTTING THE TENONS

Hold the work upright in the vise and saw down on the waste side of each tenon (fig. 49). Turn the work horizontally, and use the backsaw to remove the waste from the ends.

Use a coping saw to remove the waste between the tenons. You should cut on the line (fig. 50). The joint can then be fitted together.

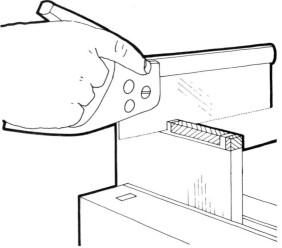

Fig. 50 Use a coping saw to remove the waste from between the tenons.

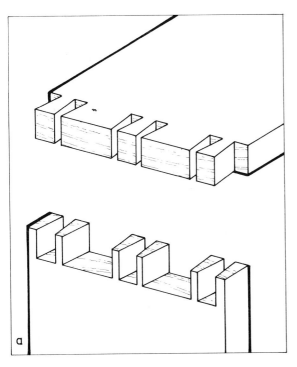

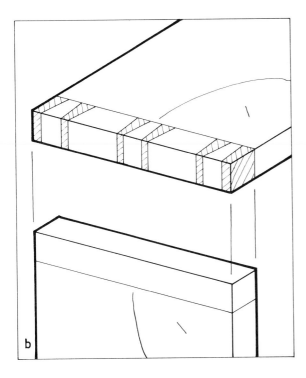

Fig. 51 The through dovetail joint: (a) completed, (b) marked-out.

THROUGH DOVETAIL JOINT

The through dovetail joint (fig. 51, a) is a strong corner joint that can be used on cabinets. The type of joint illustrated is a decorative joint that can only be cut with hand tools. Check that you have marked out the joint correctly (fig. 51, b).

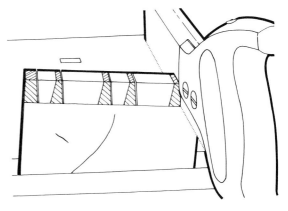

Fig. 52 Hold the wood on an angle in the vise and cut down on the lines with a dovetail saw.

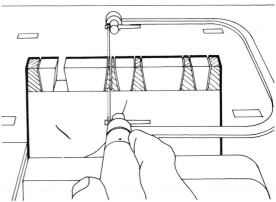

Fig. 53 Remove most of the waste from between the tails with a coping saw.

CUTTING THE TAILS

Hold the wood for the tails on an angle in the vise so that the lines to be sawn are upright. Cut on the lines with a dovetail saw (fig. 52). Reverse the angle of the wood in the vise and cut down on the remaining lines with the dovetail saw.

Hold the wood upright in the vise. Remove most of the waste from between the tails with a coping saw (fig. 53).

Clamp the wood to the bench top. Use a bevelled-edge chisel to cut halfway through the thickness of the wood, working up to the rabbet line in stages (fig. 54). You can use a mallet to tape the handle of the chisel, but take care because bevelled-edge chisels are not very strong. A piece of fibreboard (hardboard) can be used to protect the surface of the bench from accidental chisel cuts. When you have completed trimming one side, turn the work over and remove the remaining waste with the bevelled-edge chisel.

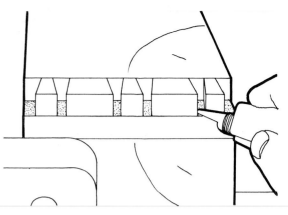

Fig. 55 Lay each set of tails over the corresponding piece of wood for the pins, and mark around the tails with a penknife.

CUTTING THE PINS

Hold the wood for the pins vertically in the vise. Cut on the waste side of the lines with a dovetail saw (fig. 56). It is important that you cut on the waste side of the lines, for this will give the joint a tight fit.

Remove most of the waste from between the pins with a coping saw. Clamp the wood to the top of the bench. Use a chisel and a mallet to cut half-way through the thickness of the wood, working up to the rabbet line in stages. Turn the work over and cut away the remaining waste.

The joint can now be fitted together. For this, hold the wood with the pins in the vise and carefully tap the tails into position using a hammer against a block of wood.

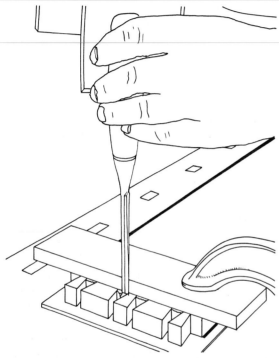

Fig. 54 Trim between the tails with a bevelled-edge chisel.

MARKING OUT THE PINS

The pins—the other half of the joint—are marked out by drawing around the tails. For this, lay each set of tails over the corresponding piece of wood for the pins and mark around the tails with a penknife (fig. 55). Rubbing blackboard chalk on the end grain of your work prior to marking-out helps to show the marks more clearly. Use a pencil and try square to square the marks down the side of the wood as far as the rabbet line. Hatch in the waste with the pencil.

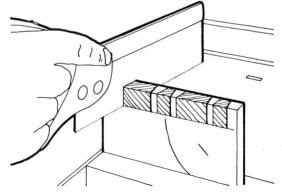

Fig. 56 Cut on the waste side of the pins with a dovetail saw.

Materials

Many people like to glue their work together, and then polish when the glue has dried. I generally work in the reverse order; that is, I polish all the inside surfaces before I glue the parts together. The reason I work this way is that the inside surfaces frequently become inaccessible and difficult to polish after gluing up. The only drawback is that I have to be careful not to get any polish on the jointing surfaces, as polish will reduce the holding power of the glue. Though I prefer to polish and then glue, you should use the system you are more successful with.

POLISHES

DANISH OIL AND TEAK OIL

These similar—but not identical—products are suitable for use on almost any wood. Of the two oils, I prefer Danish oil because it soaks further into the wood and leaves a more natural-looking finish. Both oils are easy to apply and you can achieve immediate success with either of them, as they require little skill in their application.

The oil is brushed liberally onto the wood and left for a few minutes. Then the surplus is wiped off with a rag and the surface is left to dry for about eight hours. The wood should be oiled two or three times.

Brushes that have been used for oiling can be cleaned with white alcohol. Rags that have been used for oiling must be destroyed immediately—according to the instructions printed on the can—as they can ignite spontaneously.

Furniture that has been oiled can be cleaned later with a damp rag and waxed if desired.

WHITE SHELLAC (WHITE POLISH) AND TRANSPARENT POLISH

White shellac and transparent polish can be used on any hardwood provided that the finished article will be used indoors. Both are of the French polish type; that is, they contain shellac and methylated alcohol. Of the two, I prefer transparent polish because it is clearer. They must be applied in a warm, dry atmosphere in one of two methods.

Method 1

This is the quick method. Brush a thin coat of white shellac or transparent polish onto your work, and let it dry. Drying takes about ten minutes: Then brush on a second thin coat. The second coat will take a little longer to dry than the first coat. When the white shellac or transparent polish is dry the surface is smoothed with very fine abrasive paper and is sealed with a coat of wax polish.

Method 2

This is a longer process than the first method, but it can result in a better finish. Brush on two thin coats of white shellac or transparent polish, allowing each coat to dry. Further coats are then applied with a "polishing rubber." The rubber is made by wrapping a wad of absorbent cotton about the size of a golf ball in a square of cotton cloth. Soak the absorbent cotton in white shellac or transparent polish, then squeeze until it is nearly dry. The absorbent cotton is your reservoir of polish.

Work the rubber in a small circular motion over the wood, gently squeezing the rubber to produce fresh supplies of white shellac or transparent polish when needed. One small spot of linseed oil applied to the outside of the rubber will prevent the cloth from sticking to your work. Apply several coats of shellac or polish. The last coat should be applied in straight, even strokes with a rubber soaked with methylated alcohol. When the last coat dries, smooth the surface with very fine abrasive paper.

The brushes that have been used in the polishing process can be cleaned with methylated alcohol. The polishing rubber can be stored in a glass jar with a screw-top lid.

If you get into difficulty with either of these polishing methods, allow the surface to fully harden —about two days—and rub down with fine abrasive paper. Then start the polishing process again. Make certain you are working in a warm, dry atmosphere. The polish I buy needs to be diluted about fifty percent with methylated alcohol.

Furniture that has been polished can be dusted and wax-polished occasionally.

WAX POLISH

Wax polish is bought ready-mixed in a can, with proprietary brands such as Briwax, Ronuk, and Staples being well known. It is usually applied with a soft cloth as the top coat over another finish. There is no secret about how wax should be applied: Just rub it on and polish it off.

POLYURETHANE VARNISH

This finish is not one I prefer to use on furniture, for other finishes look much better. However, if you want to use it all you have do is brush it on. Apply two or three successive coats, allowing each to dry before the next coat is applied.

There are two types of polyurethane varnish. One type comes in a single container, and the other comes in a can with a separate bottle containing the hardener. The latter type is the harder finish, but it requires an empty container in which to mix the ingredients. As always, read the mixing instructions on the can. When the last coat has hardened it can be smoothed with fine abrasive paper and polished to a brilliance with buffing cream, a substance not unlike jewellers' rouge.

GLUES

POLYVINYL ACETATE

This is the glue you will most likely use. Polyvinyl acetate is not well known by its proper name, and it is better recognized by the initials PVA. It is sold under brand names such as Evostik Resin W, Elmer's Glue, and Borden Wood Glue. PVA glue comes ready-prepared as a white liquid that can be squeezed onto the work from its flexible container. The glue sets fairly rapidly, but it is not waterproof, so do not try using it on furniture that is to be permanently placed out-of-doors. The container of glue must be stored in a frost-free environment.

To use PVA glue correctly spread a generous coating of glue over one of the joining surfaces and lightly clamp the other surface in position. Remove any surplus glue with a damp cloth before the glue sets. The joint is ready for light working within half an hour of gluing, but allow twenty-four hours for maximum strength to be attained.

UREA FORMALDEHYDE

This is the type of glue to use when you require one that's waterproof. It is hardly known by its proper name, but is known by the trade names of Cascamite and Aerolite. Cascamite is simple to apply; Aerolite has a long assembly time.

The glue requires mixing with water, so you must read the instructions on the container to find out how this should be done. Both parts of the joint have to be coated; then the joint is clamped in position for six hours. Surplus glue should be removed with a damp rag before the glue starts to set.

CONTACT ADHESIVE

Contact adhesive is commonly used for sticking plastic laminate to blockboard or chipboard, but it can be used for sticking wood, cork, rubber, metal, leather, and ceramic. It is sold under trade names such as Evostik Impact, Bostik, and Dunlop Thixofix.

To use contact adhesive correctly spread the adhesive evenly over both of the joining surfaces with either a piece of plywood or a serrated-edged spreader. These spreaders are usually supplied with the adhesive. Allow the adhesive film to touch-dry for fifteen minutes, then carefully position both surfaces and apply firm hand pressure at the center of the work, working out towards the edges. The bond will be immediate, so make sure you position the work accurately and do not trap air in the center of a panel.

EPOXY RESIN

Epoxy resin is a strong glue that is used in small

quantities to fix ceramic, glass, metal, rubber, and wood. It is sold under the trade name of Araldite. The glue is supplied in two small tubes—one tube contains resin and the other tube contains hardener.

To use epoxy resin glue correctly squeeze equal quantities from each tube and mix them thoroughly. Apply the mixture to both of the joining surfaces, then hold the surfaces together for twelve hours with sticky tape, clothespins (pegs), or small clamps. During this time a stage will be reached when the excess glue can be pared away with a sharp knife. Maximum strength in the join will be reached after three days, but moderate heat can reduce this time.

FITTINGS

Shown in the illustrations are the fittings that were used in the construction of all the items described in this book. Detailed explanations of these fittings are not required, as their applications are fairly obvious. Look at all the hardware stocks in your area, as the design of fittings is continuously changing. With some searching you may be able to find just what you require.

FLATHEAD (COUNTERSINK) SCREW

The flathead screw (fig. 57, a) is available in a range of lengths from 3/8 in (9 mm) to 3 in (75 mm). It is also available in a range of thicknesses called the gauge number of the screw. A useful thickness of screw is no. eight gauge; a thicker screw would be no. ten gauge and a thinner screw would be a no. six gauge. Short screws have a lower gauge number.

Screws are also available in a variety of metals and finishes. A strong screw is a steel screw with a bright, zinc-plated anticorrosive finish. A brass screw is less strong, but looks better on high-class work.

When ordering screws state the quantity, the type of head, the length, the gauge number, and the metal or finish required.

Be careful when fitting a flathead screw. First drill the clearance hole (fig. 58, a). Select the drill size from the following table.

Second, drill the pilot hole (fig. 58, b)—the correct size can be found in the table. Third,

gauge number	clearance hole	pilot hole
4	1/8 in (3 mm)	5/64 in (2 mm)
6	5/32 in (4 mm)	5/64 in (2 mm)
8	3/16 in (5 mm)	3/32 in (2.5 mm)
10	7/32 in (5.5 mm)	1/8 in (3 mm)
12	1/4 in (6 mm)	1/8 in (3 mm)

countersink the clearance hole so that the head of the screw will fit flush (fig. 58, c). Fourth, insert the screw with a screwdriver that fits the head of the screw (fig. 58, d). Be careful with brass screws, for the heads can snap off. Some grease can be used on the screws as a lubricant.

CHIPBOARD SCREW

The chipboard screw (fig. 57, b) is threaded along its entire length. This type of screw should be used when working in chipboard, as it grips better than the ordinary type of screw and is less likely to split the wood.

BLOCK JOINT FITTINGS

Block joint fittings (fig. 57, c) can make you feel very creative, for with these you can assemble a large chipboard construction in just a few hours. Screw the parts of this joint to the separate panels; to fix the panels tighten the bolt that holds the joint together.

SCREW COVER-HEADS

Screw cover-heads (fig. 57, d & fig. 57, e) are available in white or brown plastic and provide a neat finish.

PIANO HINGE

The piano hinge (fig. 57, f) is available in plastic, steel, or brass. The brass hinge looks best on high-class work, but is expensive. I like to polish the knuckle of a brass hinge before fitting the hinge to the work.

MAGNETIC CATCHES

Magnetic catches (fig. 57, g) work well, are easy to fit, and have no alignment problems.

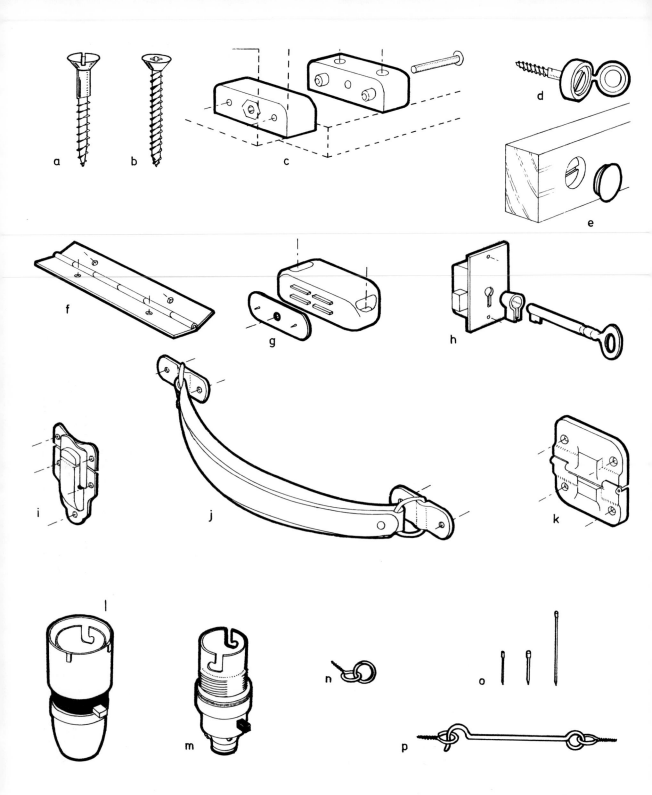

Fig. 57 Fittings: (a) flathead screw, (b) chipboard screw, (c) block joint fittings, (d) & (e) screw cover-heads, (f) piano hinge, (g) magnetic catch, (h) lock, (i) briefcase catch, (j) briefcase handle, (k) brief-

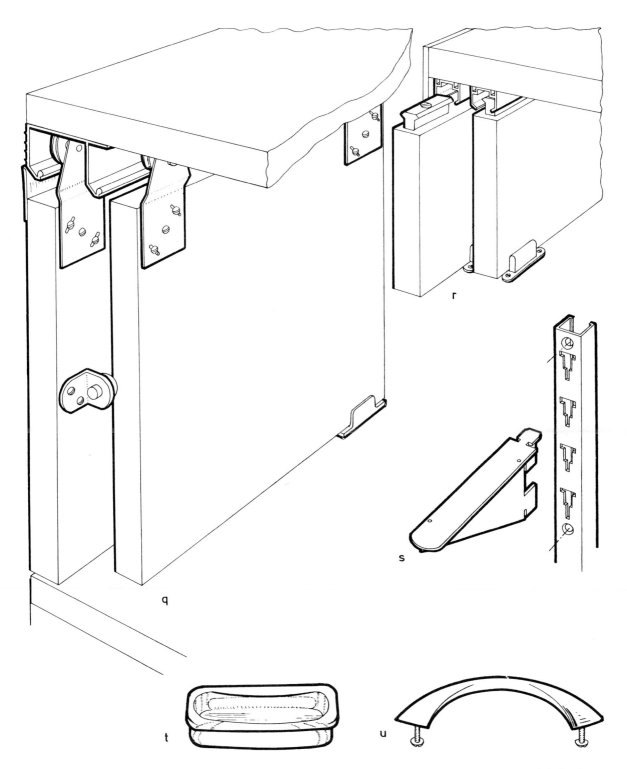

case hinge, (l) lamp-fitting in plastic, (m) lamp-fitting in metal, (n) picture-frame screw eyes, (o) brads (panel pins), (p) cabin hook, (q) & (r) sliding-door mechanisms, (s) adjustable shelving, (t) & (u) handles.

LOCKS

Locks (fig. 57, h) require careful fitting if they are to work well and look good. When fitting a lock, the first decision you have to make is where to drill the hole for the key. The escutcheon—the brass keyhole shape—is tapped against the wood with a hammer to mark the amount of wood that must be removed. Use a drill and a coping saw to make this shape. The escutcheon can be fixed permanently in position with epoxy resin glue.

BRIEFCASE FITTINGS

The briefcase catch (fig. 57, i), the handle (fig. 57, j), and the hinge (fig. 57, k) are fitted to the work with chromium-plated screws.

LAMP FITTINGS

Lamp fittings are available in plastic (fig. 57, l) and in metal (fig. 57, m). The metal type must be used when a metal support column is incorporated into the design because the metal column must be grounded (earthed). Take care to wire the fitting correctly; if you are unsure about how to do this seek advice from a competent electrician.

PICTURE-FRAME SCREW EYES

Picture-frame screw eyes (fig. 57, n) are needed to fix the hanging wire or hanging cord to a picture frame.

BRADS (PANEL PINS)

Small nails (fig. 57, o) are commonly called brads (panel pins), and are sold in sizes from ½ in (12 mm) to 1 in (25 mm).

CABIN HOOK

The cabin hook (fig. 57, p) is an old-fashioned device, but it is still useful today.

SLIDING-DOOR MECHANISM

The sliding-door mechanism (fig. 57, q) is useful when hanging doors made of melamine-faced chip-board. I have glued a wide strip of flexible plastic to the top of the door in order to conceal the track. A sliding-door mechanism with sliders is also shown (fig. 57, r). The sliders fix into holes in the edge of the chipboard door; PVA glue is used in the holes to make the fixing secure.

ADJUSTABLE SHELVING

Adjustable shelving (fig. 57, s) looks smart in aluminium. The uprights need screwing to a wall at frequent intervals. The shelf-supports latch into slots already cut in the uprights.

HANDLES

A wooden handle (fig. 57, t) looks attractive when made of teak, but it needs to be glued into a shallow rabbet. The shape of the rabbet is easy to mark out if you first make a cardboard template.

An easier handle to fit is the metal or plastic type (fig. 57, u). You may have some difficulty in spacing the holes for the bolts. However, if you drill the holes slightly oversize it increases the tolerance with which you work.

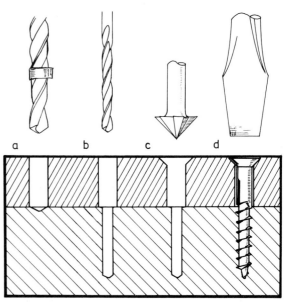

Fig. 58 Fitting a flathead screw: (a) drill the clearance hole, (b) drill the pilot hole, (c) countersink the clearance hole, (d) insert the screw.

Upholstery

Upholstery used to be a separate trade, but it can now be part of woodworking. Nowadays, with the use of rubber webbing and foam cushioning, the task of upholstery is much easier. It is largely a question of learning the basic skills, and of approaching the work from the right direction.

THE MATERIALS

THE FRAME

Traditionally, beechwood has always been used for a chair frame, but almost any sound hardwood can be used if it holds tacks well. The separate parts of the frame are better dowel-jointed together rather than mortise-and-tenoned, as dowel joints will take tacks in all places.

It is important that the sharp edges of a frame are rounded over to about $\frac{1}{8}$-in (3-mm) radius, because the sharp edges of a frame can cut through the upholstery fabric as the chair is put to use. You can round over the sharp edges with a rasp or coarse abrasive paper.

TACKS AND STAPLES

Upholstery fabrics can be fastened to the frame with $\frac{3}{8}$-in (9-mm) upholstery tacks, but a neater and quicker job can be done with staples fired from a staple gun (fig. 59, a). The staple gun needs to be fitted with $\frac{3}{8}$-in (9-mm) hardened steel staples.

Some of the tacks or staples must be removed in order to achieve the required shape, evenness, and firmness in the upholstery. To remove tacks or staples use a mallet and a screwdriver.

RUBBER WEBBING

Rubber webbing is used to form the base of almost all seating units. The webbing is 2 in (50 mm) wide, and it is stretched across a frame with 2-in (50-mm) wide spaces between the strands of webbing.

One end of the webbing is attached to the frame with three $\frac{5}{8}$-in (16-mm) webbing tacks—very large-headed tacks—or with three $\frac{5}{8}$-in (16-mm) clout roofing nails. The webbing is then stretched across the frame until a predrawn line across the

Table of initial tensions

The seat span is the distance between the tacks or grooves. The table shows the strand length to be marked on the webbing before it is stretched. The tacks will be placed about $\frac{3}{8}$ in (9 mm) inside this marked length.

seat span	hard	medium	soft
18 in (457 mm)	16½ in (419 mm)	17 in (432 mm)	17½ in (444 mm)
19 in (483 mm)	17½ in (444 mm)	18 in (457 mm)	18½ in (470 mm)
20 in (508 mm)	18½ in (470 mm)	19 in (483 mm)	19½ in (495 mm)
21 in (533 mm)	19½ in (495 mm)	20 in (508 mm)	20½ in (521 mm)
22 in (559 mm)	20 in (508 mm)	20½ in (521 mm)	21½ in (546 mm)
23 in (584 mm)	21 in (533 mm)	21½ in (546 mm)	22 in (559 mm)
24 in (610 mm)	22 in (559 mm)	22½ in (571 mm)	23 in (584 mm)

webbing (*see* table of initial tensions) is in line with the outer edge of the frame. Insert three more webbing tacks or clout nails to secure the strand of webbing to the frame, then cut the webbing from the roll with scissors.

On show-wood frames, such as a fireside chair, neat metal clips can be used to attach the webbing to the frame. The clips are clamped to the end of the webbing with a metalworker's vise. Each clip should slide into a groove or slot in the frame that has been cut $5/32$ in (4 mm) wide and $9/16$ in (15 mm) deep, and at an angle of 75° (fig. 59, b). If you do not have the equipment to cut this groove, screw each clip to the frame with a steel roundhead screw 1 in (25 mm) long × no. six gauge.

UPHOLSTERY FOAM

The foam that you buy must be of upholstery density. Cut on either a handsaw or a knife or hacksaw blade, which are a little more difficult.

A firm foam called reconstituted foam is needed for a seat with a solid base, with a secondary layer of normal density upholstery foam glued on top. Special glues are available for gluing foams together, but you can get away with contact adhesive.

FIRST COVERING

The foam needs a first covering with unbleached calico, muslin, or cotton sheeting, to shield the foam from the light and to protect the top covering from the thread-drawing effects of the foam. This first covering will also give you the opportunity to practice your upholstery skills, and help to shape up some of the snags.

WADDING

A layer of wadding, linterfelt, or Dacron™ sandwiched between the first covering and the top covering helps to plump up the upholstery, and give it a more satisfactory appearance and a warmer feel. The thickness of the wadding can be increased slightly at the seat corners. You can feather the wadding along the edges by pulling some of it away; the wadding you gain can be used for stuffing the corners.

TOP COVERING

The top covering can be of plastic, leather, Draylon™, Naugahyde™, or any closely woven material. Materials with bold patterns are the hardest to fit because of the problems of matching and aligning the pattern.

All woven materials have a pile that smooths in one direction. You must stroke the material with your hand to find the direction of the pile. The material should then be fitted with the pile direction as shown (fig. 59, c).

Materials can be marked out on the back with tailor's chalk, allowing $1/2$ in (12 mm) for turning in at the edges or for seaming. Woven materials can be torn to shape across the weave, and cut in the direction of the weave with scissors.

First, fix the top covering at the centers of the four sides; then work towards the corners using tacks or staples at frequent intervals. The method of pleating at a corner is shown (fig. 59, d).

HAND-SEWING

Any hand-sewing is carried out by slip-stitching with a curved upholstery needle (fig. 59, e). These needles are currently easily obtainable from department stores (high-street stores). Use extra-strong, twisted thread (sewing twist) for your work that is either of the same shade as the top covering or slightly darker than the top covering; this way your stitches will blend into the fabric.

CUSHIONS

Upholstery foam can be easily inserted into cushions made up with a zip-along one-edge. At a later stage, the foam can be removed so that the outer covering can be washed or dry-cleaned. Notice from the illustrations in Part Two that cushions can have walls, or the top and bottom panels can be brought together and seamed halfway down the sides. If you are unable to machine-stitch, then an upholsterer will gladly make up the cushions for you. You can find the addresses of upholsterers in the Yellow Pages.

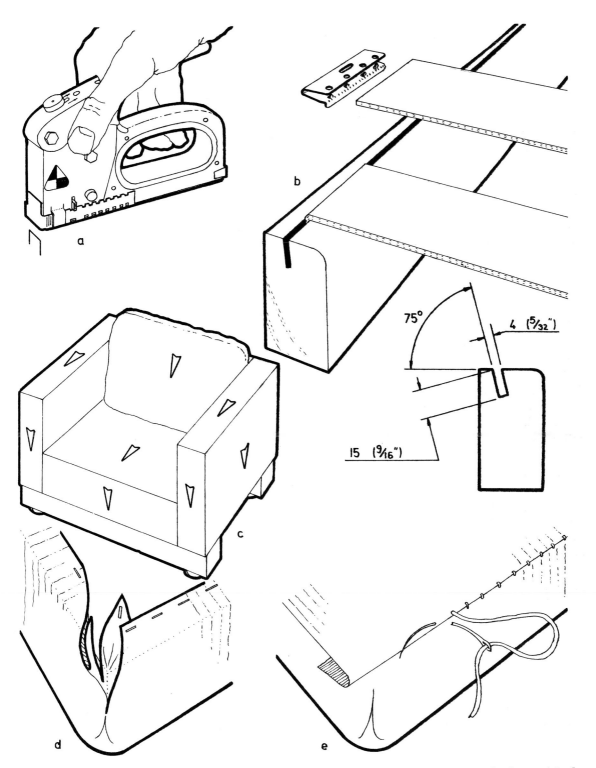

75°

4 (5/32")

15 (9/16")

Fig. 59 Upholstery: (a) staple gun, (b) using metal clips to attach rubber webbing to the frame, (c) the direction of the pile on a chair, (d) the method of pleating at a corner, (e) slip-stitching with a curved upholstery needle.

Safety in the Workshop

Safety is an important aspect of practical work. Here I explain the safety aspects for five important parts of the body. If you notice omissions it is up to you to incorporate them into your working methods.

THE HANDS

The workshop should be warm because cold hands are less sensitive to hand and machine tools. Of the hand tools, it is the chisel and the saw that are potentially the most dangerous if wrongly or carelessly used. Make sure these tools are sharp, the wood is held securely, you stand correctly, and that the position of your hands is correct. Of the woodworking machinery, it is the power saws and the planing machines that are potentially the most dangerous. If either of these machines is installed in your workshop you must make every effort to become familiar with the machinery before switching it on. It may be a good idea to be able to lock each machine—or the electric power to the workshop—so that inexperienced members of the family cannot use it without your knowledge.

Circular saws

The position of the circular saw in your workshop is important, as ample space is needed for the moving of lumber. However, a space should not be made for the saw at the expense of finding a satisfactory position for the bench.

The saw should be well guarded, satisfactorily equipped, and well maintained. On no account should the guard be removed from the saw. The saw blade should be properly sharpened and set, and it should be regularly checked for cracks—particularly near the gullets of the teeth. A cracked saw should not be used. A saw blade should be correctly tensioned by the manufacturer. Without the correct tension the blade will not run true, and will not cut accurately. If, by any means, a saw blade becomes overheated it should be returned to the manufacturer for retensioning.

A properly shaped push-stick should always be on hand when sawing; use this rather than your hand to push wood past the saw blade.

Machine planer

When a machine planer is installed the correct setting of the blades in the cutter block is very important; $\frac{1}{32}$ in (.75 mm) is the maximum projection for each blade from the cutter block. The blades must be kept sharp, and they should be periodically despatched for regrinding and balancing.

Wood should not be forced through the machine or planed against the grain; neither should short pieces of wood be machine-planed. A guard over the cutter block of the machine should be used in the correct manner (i.e., set to just clear the thickness of the wood), and the part of the cutter block that is exposed behind the fence should be well guarded. The belt guard from the motor to the cutter block should also be guarded.

Bandsaws

A bandsaw should have the blade completely guarded except between the table and the top guide. The top guide should be adjustable, and it should be set each time the saw is used so that it just clears the thickness of the material. The bottom mouth of the bandsaw should be replaced when it becomes worn. The belt drive from the motor to the machine should be guarded.

THE EYES

In any operation where wood chips, dust or other particles may become airborne, then one-piece PVC goggles or safety spectacles should be worn. They are easy to see through, and quite inexpensive.

THE EARS

Some machine tools make a great deal of noise,

and the noise level becomes more evident if the machines are operated in a small workshop. Working conditions can be made more tolerable when ear protectors are worn. A local wood machinist has told me that the cheaper types of ear protectors are suitable because a certain amount of sound penetration is required in order that the machines can be operated safely.

Of course, ear protectors may solve the problem of excessive noise for the operator, but they do not solve the problem of noise that is an annoyance to neighbors. Noisy machinery can become a nuisance to others; either have all your machining done by a factory that is away from your neighborhood or choose a part of the day when the operation of machinery will be the least inconvenient to others.

THE HAIR

You should not operate any machine tool if you have long, uncontrolled hair. The technical college near my home makes its students, male and female, wear snoods. You may find that an elastic band makes a cheaper alternative.

THE NOSE AND RESPIRATORY PASSAGES

The dust from certain hardwood lumber (*see* Appendix B) can irritate the nose and upper respiratory passages. The machining of these woods is best avoided.

PART II
Projects

Design

THE NEW APPROACH

It is common practice in schools for design and technology to be taught using three materials—wood, metal, and plastic. However, it is my intention that we make use of the new approach towards design that uses wood as the main constructional material.

Here, then, are the steps in design and technology. I wish to thank Jim Patterson for his patience in explaining them to me.

DESIGN AND TECHNOLOGY

THE BRIEF

Start off by writing a short brief that states what it is that is to be made, and either by whom the object is to be used or where it is to be used. You can also, if you wish, state the materials from which the object is to be made. For example:

Design and make a holder for twenty cassettes 4⅜ (110 mm) × 2¾ in (70 mm) × ¾ in (18 mm). The holder is to be suitable for a young person's room, and must be made mainly from wood.

DESIGN ANALYSIS

Here you must list the requirements of the design. Each statement should be a strong positive point; it helps to include the word "must" in every statement. For example:

a) *it must be stable*
b) *it must be attractive*
c) *it must be easy to select a cassette*

POSSIBLE SOLUTIONS TO EACH DESIGN ANALYSIS PROBLEM

Here you refer to problem a) in your design analysis, and write down as many possible ways as you can think of for solving this problem. Then you do the same thing for problem b), and continue until you reach the end of your design analysis statements.
For example:

a) *have four legs*
have three legs
have two parallel runners
have two runners crossing each other
have a flat base
b) *be made from an attractive wood*
have polished surfaces
have textured surfaces

SYNTHESIS OF THE BEST SOLUTIONS TO EACH DESIGN ANALYSIS PROBLEM

Make perspective sketches with brief notes explaining the advantages, disadvantages, and method of construction of each design. Each sketch should be numbered, and should be a development of the previous sketch. When you run out of developing ideas, continue with a fresh idea; preconceived ideas should not have overriding importance.

PRODUCTION OF A WORKING DRAWING

Your best design should be chosen so that from it you can produce a working drawing. Ideally, your working drawing will be full-size, but if the object is large you can reproduce it at one-eighth (one-tenth) scale.

REALIZATION OF THE DESIGN

Here you can either construct the article or make a prototype.

EVALUATION

Finally, you can evaluate your success by com-

This sturdy briefcase is made mostly of plywood: It can be covered on the outside in either vinyl or leather, and lined on the inside with baize.

A toy tractor and van built along similar lines. Both can be made of various pieces of lumber.

Picture framing is a practical craft that can be accomplished in a few simple steps.

Silver, glass and porcelain can be displayed in a corner cabinet. The baize-covered panels in the back of the cabinet make an attractive background.

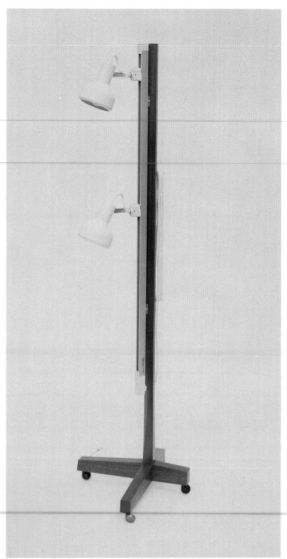

This adjustable standard lamp uses a lighting unit similar to those used in store window displays, and can be raised or lowered, as well as swivelled and tilted.

Three unique table lamps that can be built with scrap pieces of lumber and decorated with leather, vinyl or fabric.

*This beautiful tile-top table is designed along the
lines of classical simplicity.*

*This comfortable, low-back car-
ver chair has curved-back rails
and a dished seat. Four buttons
covered with leather lend a nice
decorative touch.*

*A tv table is a practical household
addition.*

C

A recliner chair with an inner frame that is made from hardwood, and fitted with rubber webbing.

A fireside chair of open framework construction and Scandinavian appearance. The seat and back cushions are identical, and can be fitted with covers that can be unzipped.

paring the finished article with the design brief and with your own design analysis. How successful is it? Does it stand up to criticism?

Look at some of the articles that I have made, and evaluate them. If you are a beginner you may want to copy some of these articles until you become used to woodworking; ultimately, you will progress towards designing articles that you can make. Here is a short list of articles that you could consider for designing and making:

kitchen equipment
boxes
cupboards
lamps
tables
stools
chests
picture frames
toys
holders
racks
a settee
garden furniture
tools
games

A SKETCH BOOK

Clearly, design and technology offer a stream-lined approach towards design that might make better sense in the educational setting than it does to an individual designer. However, it is not an approach that should be shunned, since it has been used with good results.

When I am designing I like to use an artist's spiral-bound sketch book that is 14 in × 10 in (350 mm × 250 mm). Because it is spiral-bound the pages can be folded back flat, so that I can even sit up in bed and draw if I want.

Sketch even if you consider yourself a poor sketcher; after all, the purpose of a sketch is simply to record ideas you don't want to forget. I like to make perspective sketches, but sometimes I make measured drawings. I also like to record important facts in my sketch book—such as the overall dimensions and the cutting list of the materials required. Sometimes inspired ideas come when I am sitting at the fireside; I doodle these on the backs of used envelopes, and later stick them into my book.

A sketch book makes a good source of reference, as each sketch is always drawn with a certain idea in mind—even though it might not lead to something being made. From time to time I am inspired by one idea that I feel I have to follow through on. Sometimes ideas are borrowed from other people, and developed in an evolutionary process. If you copy some of the articles described in this book you should make changes and carry out improvements before you start the construction.

Woodworking Without Tears

This chapter tells you how to overcome some of the frustrations you may meet as a beginner.

READ THE INSTRUCTIONS FULLY

Read the instructions fully before you start and make sure that you understand what you will have to do.

DO NOT WORK IN BOTH METRIC AND IMPERIAL MEASUREMENTS

This book has been written so that you can work in either millimeters or in inches. Do not try working in both units of measurement or you will become confused. In the text we have placed the imperial measurements first, then the metric measurements. For the convenience of those who are more familiar with the metric system, the metric measurements (in millimeters) are first in the diagram, and the imperial measurements second.

DO NOT BE OVERAMBITIOUS IN THE BEGINNING

If you are working alone choose something for your first project that is a little below your capabilities. That way you should achieve success fairly readily—and there is nothing like success to spur you on.

BUY YOUR WOOD READY DRESSED (READY MACHINE-PLANED)

Buy your wood ready dressed (ready machine-planed) to the sizes shown in the cutting list. The extra expense of machine-planing is small compared with the effort that hand-planing requires.

IDENTIFY EACH PIECE OF WOOD

Identify each piece of wood—with a pencil mark if necessary—before you start construction.

MARK WITH FACE-SIDE AND FACE-EDGE MARKS

Mark the two best surfaces on each piece of wood with reference marks; the larger surface is called the face-side and the smaller surface is called the face-edge (fig. 60). A pencil is used to make these marks.

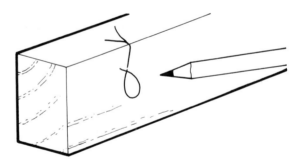

Fig. 60 *The larger surface is called the face-side and the smaller surface is called the face-edge.*

ARRANGE THE PIECES

Arrange each piece of wood so that the two best surfaces will show on the outside of the finished piece of furniture.

PENCIL OR KNIFE

Make pencil marks where guidance is required, and make knife lines where accurate cuts have to be made.

CHECK TWICE; CUT ONCE!

Check your marking-out twice, and cut once. Usually it is very difficult to glue pieces back on again once you have cut them off.

HOLD THE WOOD IN THE VISE

Hold the wood firmly either in the vise, or on the top of the bench with bench dogs or a C clamp. Do not hold the wood with your hands as you work.

CUT ON THE WASTE SIDES OF THE LINES

Cut joints on the waste sides of the lines so that the joints are a tight fit.

CLEAN UP CAREFULLY

Remove a fine shaving from the surface of the wood using a smoothing plane with a sharp, finely set blade.

USE ABRASIVE PAPER SPARINGLY

Try to achieve a finish using the smoothing plane rather than large amounts of abrasive paper.

ASSEMBLE THE WORK DRY

Put the work together without glue to see that everything fits well. Make adjustments where necessary. Consider how you will tackle the gluing up.

GLUE UP QUICKLY

Gluing is a critical stage, and needs adequate preparation. Among the things needed are: clamps that are ready for use, a damp rag to wipe off excess glue, and tapes to check for squareness. If necessary, get someone to help you with the gluing up. Spread the glue, then clamp the work together by using large pieces of waste wood between the shoes of the clamps and the surface of your work. The waste wood will prevent the metal shoes from damaging your work.

CAREFULLY CHECK FOR SQUARENESS AND FLATNESS

Check for the squareness by ensuring that the diagonal measurements across your work are equal. Check for flatness by sighting across your work. Carefully bend your work or move the clamp shoes slightly until all is correct. Wipe away the excess glue with a damp rag or sponge.

IF YOUR POLISHING FAILS

If your attempts at polishing fail give the surface several days to harden, clean off the polish with abrasive paper, and start the polishing process again. Remember that a warm, dry atmosphere is usually needed to achieve success with polishing.

WHEN SOMETHING GOES WRONG

Bear in mind that beginners can have beginner's luck, but sometimes beginners meet circumstances that an expert might find hard to correct. If things do go wrong, then stop, read through the instructions again, and think about what you have done. If necessary, put things off for another day when you may have fresh thoughts on the matter.

FOR MAXIMUM PLEASURE AND MINIMUM STRESS

To enjoy the benefits of woodworking and furniture making—and avoid stress—woodworkers should learn to pace themselves. Some people have a naturally easy pace when they work, while others strain unnecessarily. Making furniture by hand is a long term process. A fairly simple chair could take several weeks of full-time work, but if the work is being undertaken through adult education classes it could take a year or longer. Be prepared to take your time, and be advised that craftwork that is rushed is not craftwork at all.

Simple Workshop Aids

I am including this section because I am certain beginning woodworkers want to know something about the traditions of woodworking and the ways in which woodshop problems were solved in the past. There follows in this chapter advice on: a) racking tools, b) protecting your oilstone from dust, damage, and uneven wear, c) supporting wood on top of the bench when sawing to length, d) supporting wood when planing end grain, and e) supporting wood when cutting a miter.

A TOOL RACK

One of the first workshop aids that is needed is a rack in which to store your tools. Here is just one solution to the problem (fig. 61, a). This rack will hold two rules, a try square, a spokeshave, four chisels, a hammer, and a mallet. Furthermore, the rack is portable so you can carry it to a job indoors, hang it from the end of the bench, stand it in the tool well, or hang it on the workshop wall.

You may like to redesign this rack, re-organize it, or design another rack along similar lines to hold your planes and gauges. Remember, though, that any rack you make should protect the sharp edges of the tools from damage, be a convenient place to put the tools when they are not in use, and make each tool easy to find when it is needed. As you can see, I have done the design analysis for you!

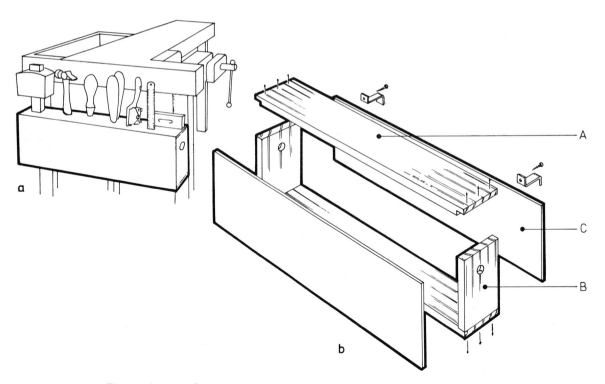

Fig. 61 A tool rack: (a) completed, (b) an exploded view of the construction.

Softwood

key	description	quantity	length	width	thickness
A	top & bottom	2	24 in (610 mm)	3¾ in (95 mm)	⅝ in (16 mm)
B	ends	2	7 in (180 mm)	3¾ in (95 mm)	⅝ in (16 mm)

Fibreboard (hardboard)

C	front & back	2	24 in (610 mm)	7½ in (190 mm)	⅛ in (3 mm)

CONSTRUCTION

An exploded view of the construction (fig. 61, b) shows that the corners are fastened with an end rabbet joint (lap butt joint) that is fixed with glue and nails, and that the front and back are glued and nailed in position.

1) Hold the two end pieces together in the vise and mark to length with a knife (fig. 62). Remove the pieces from the vise and square the knife lines around the wood. Hatch in the waste with a pencil.

2) Hold the top and bottom pieces together in the vise and mark to length with a knife (fig. 63). Square the knife marks around each piece and hatch in the waste with a pencil.

3) Cut off the waste from the ends with a backsaw.

4) Arrange the pieces as they will be on the finished article (fig. 64). Position the face sides—the best surfaces—on the outside. You should use the numbering system illustrated here, for it shows at one time: a) the outside surfaces, b) the front edges, and c) the adjacent joints. None of these pencilled marks need be removed until after the joints have been glued together.

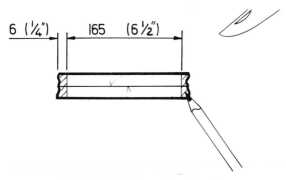

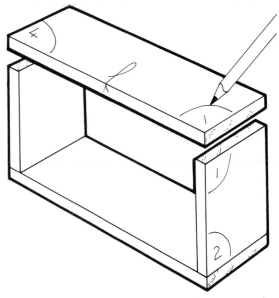

Fig. 62 Mark the ends to length.

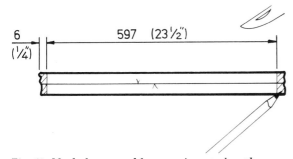

Fig. 63 Mark the top and bottom pieces to length.

Fig. 64 Arrange the parts as they will appear on the finished rack, and number the joints.

5) Set a cutting gauge to just over the thickness of the end pieces, then gauge a rabbet line across the inside surfaces on the long pieces (fig. 65).

69

Set a marking gauge to one-third the thickness of the wood, and use this setting to gauge the depth of the joint across the end grain. Hatch in the waste with a pencil (fig. 66).

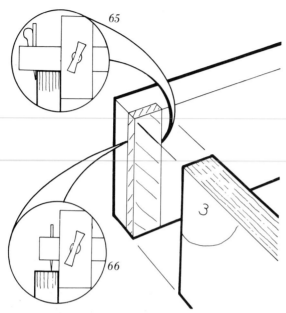

Fig. 65 Use a cutting gauge set to the thickness of the end pieces to gauge a rabbet line across the inside surfaces on the top and bottom pieces.

Fig. 66 Use a marking gauge set to one-third the thickness of the wood to gauge the depth of the joint.

6) Cut the end rabbet joint in the usual way (*see* figs. 35–37).

7) Space the tools on top of the rack and mark out shapes for each tool.

8) Holes which are of an irregular shape can be cut with a coping saw. To do this, first drill a ¼-in (6-mm) hole through the waste, thread the coping saw blade through the hole, then reattach the saw blade to the frame of the coping saw.

Small slots for tools will have to be chopped with a mallet and chisel (*see* chopping a mortise, fig. 39). Here the marking-out must be done on both sides of the wood; then you can cut halfway into the wood from both sides, resulting in a clean hole.

9) Drill a 1-in (25-mm) diameter finger hole in each end piece. To do this, drill through the wood until the point of the bit emerges on the far side.

Then turn the wood around and drill into the hole from the back: This will result in a very clean finish.

10) When all the shapes have been cut and cleaned up—a piece of abrasive paper wrapped around a dowel will help here—and checked for size against each tool, then the parts can be glued together.

Tap three brads (panel pins) partly into each joint. Glue one surface of the joint, then tap the brads home. It helps if part of the work is held in the vise. A hammer and nail set (panel pin punch) can be used to sink the heads of the brads just below the surface.

Check the assembly for squareness by seeing that the diagonals are of the same length.

Give the job a gentle push to make any correction that is required.

Wipe away the surplus glue from around the joints with a damp rag, and leave the assembly overnight for the glue to dry.

11) Level the edges of the rack with a plane as preparation for fitting the fibreboard (hardboard).

12) If contact adhesive is used to glue the fibreboard in position there is no need to use any brads, but if PVA glue is used you will have to use ¾-in (19-mm) × 16 gauge brads to attach the fibreboard to the assembly.

13) Clean up the whole of the outside of the rack with a smoothing plane. The edges of the fibreboard can be planed, but never plane the surface of fibreboard. The ends of the rack must be planed from the edges into the middle; otherwise, the joints will split away. Round off all sharp corners.

14) You may wish to polish the rack as I did, with one coat of Danish oil and one coat of wax.

OILSTONE CASE

I found an oilstone case, similar to the one illustrated here (fig. 67), among the tools I inherited. The original concept of making a case for the oilstone is a very old one. The reason for making a case is that it protects the oilstone from dust, accidental damage, drying out, and if the oilstone is provided with hardwood run-off blocks it prevents the oilstone from being worn unevenly.

Hardwood

key	description	quantity	length	width	thickness
A	body	2	10½ in (270 mm)	2¾ in (70 mm)	1¼ in (30 mm)
B	end blocks	2	1½ in (38 mm)	2 in (51 mm)	½ in (12 mm)

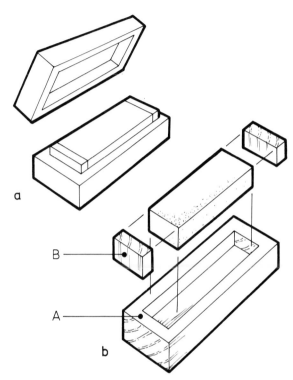

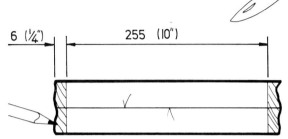

Fig. 68 *Mark the pieces for the body to length.*

Fig. 67 *An oilstone case: (a) completed, (b) an exploded view of the construction.*

CONSTRUCTION

1) Hold the two pieces for the body together in the vise. Mark to length with a knife, and hatch in the waste with a pencil (fig. 68). Take the pieces from the vise, and square the knife lines around each piece.

2) Place each piece on the bench hook, and cut the waste from the ends with a backsaw.

3) Place your oilstone on the middle of one of the pieces. Check the position of the oilstone with a ruler, then draw around the oilstone with a pencil. The rectangle you have drawn must be lengthened at each end by ½ in (12 mm) for the run-off blocks. Mark out the second piece of wood in the same way.

4) You can use either a large center bit in a hand brace or a large spade bit (flatbit) in an electric pillar drill to bore out the waste to a depth of half the thickness of the oilstone—about 9/16 in (14 mm). Whichever method of drilling you use, make sure that the point of the bit does not pass right through the work.

5) Chop out the remaining waste with a mallet and chisel: Take care to use the chisel across the grain, as you could split your wood.

6) Fit the end blocks with the end grain uppermost. The reason for fitting them this way is that the end grain is the hardest part of the wood. The blocks must fit flush with the surface of the oilstone.

7) Make the lid a loose fit over the oilstone.

8) Put the lid on the oilstone and clean up the outside surfaces with a smoothing plane. Take particular care not to split the ends of the wood (*see* Shooting Board).

9) A small chamfer—an angle of 45°—around the top edge of the lid helps to distinguish the lid from the base. Mark out this chamfer with two parallel pencil lines about ⅛ in (3 mm) from the edge of

the wood. Make this shape using a smoothing plane held at an angle.

In case you find this oilstone case old-fashioned, I have included a drawing of a more modern version (fig. 69).

BENCH HOOK

This is a very simple aid (fig. 70), and yet a very useful one, for it is used to support wood on top of the bench when you are cutting across the grain with a backsaw. It should be made from a hardwood such as beech or oak.

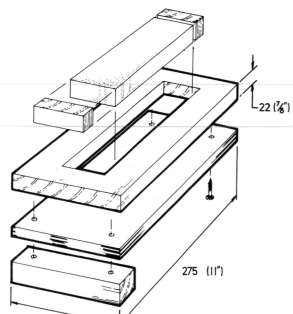

Fig. 69 An alternative oilstone case.

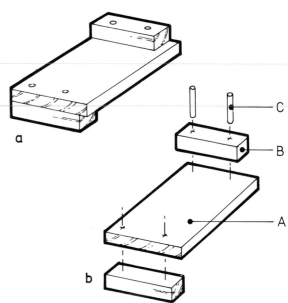

Fig. 70 The bench hook: (a) completed for right-handed use, (b) an exploded view of the construction.

CONSTRUCTION

1) Note that no allowance for waste has been made in the cutting list, as the size of a bench hook is generally immaterial; therefore, the construction

CUTTING LIST FOR BENCH HOOK—planed, finished sizes

Hardwood

key	description	quantity	length	width	thickness
A	base	1	8 in (200 mm)	5 in (130 mm)	½ in (12 mm)
B	stops	2	4½ in (118 mm)	1¼ in (32 mm)	⅞ in (23 mm)

Beechwood dowel

C		1	8 in (200 mm)	½-in (12-mm) diameter	

can start without woodworkers having to mark and cut pieces to length.

2) Place each stop in the position it will later occupy, and draw around it with a pencil. This indicates the gluing area. Woodworkers who are left-handed will have to fix the stops in reverse to those in the illustration.

3) Glue the base with PVA glue, then press the stops in position. Use the vise and a C clamp to hold the work until the glue has set. When the C clamp is used, scrap blocks of wood should be placed between the shoes and the work as this a) prevents the shoe on the clamp from denting your work, and b) helps to spread the pressure from the clamp along the joint. Surplus glue should be removed with a damp rag before the glue sets.

4) When the glue has hardened the clamps can be removed. Measure the positions for the dowels, and mark these positions with a cross on the stops using a pencil.

5) Place the wood low in the vise. Use a brace and ½-in (12-mm) bit to bore the holes for the dowels. Bore through the wood until the point of the bit emerges, then turn the wood around and bore back into the holes: This method will result in a clean hole. As an alternative to a brace and bit, a ½-in (12-mm) spade bit (flatbit) and electric pillar drill could be used.

6) Saw the dowels to finish a little longer than required. Cover the surface of your bench with paper to protect it from glue. Glue the dowels and the holes well. Tap the dowels into the holes with a hammer.

7) Allow the glue to set, then trim the dowels flush with the work with a sharp, finely set smoothing plane.

SHOOTING BOARD

This aid supports your wood when you are planing the end grain (fig. 71); without a shooting board the end grain will split. The construction has been simplified from the traditional method by using two pieces of blockboard glued together to form the body.

CONSTRUCTION

1) Plane one long edge true on the platform. This will form the edge of the rabbet. Position the platform over the base, and draw a line along the true edge to mark the extent of the gluing area. If you are left-handed, reverse the way it is shown in the illustration.

2) Glue the base, then clamp the base and platform together until the glue has set.

3) Mark and cut the stops to length so that they accurately fit the work.

4) Place the stops in position, and draw around each of them with a pencil to mark the extent of the gluing area. Glue the stops and hold them in position with the vise and a C clamp. Check carefully that the stops are square before you leave them overnight for the glue to dry.

5) Measure and mark out the dowel positions.

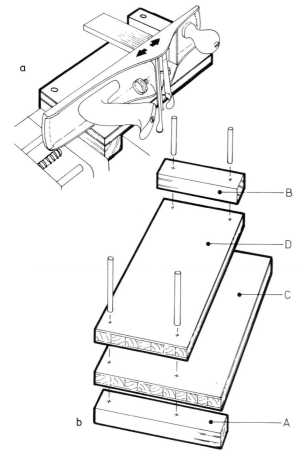

Fig. 71 The shooting board: (a) completed for right-handed use, (b) an exploded view of the construction.

Hardwood

key	description	quantity	length	width	thickness
A	stop	1	7½ in (190 mm)	1½ in (38 mm)	1 in (25 mm)
B	stop	1	5½ in (140 mm)	1½ in (38 mm)	1 in (25 mm)

Blockwood

key	description	quantity	length	width	thickness
C	base	1	11 in (280 mm)	7 in (180 mm)	¾ in (19 mm)
D	platform	1	11 in (280 mm)	5 in (130 mm)	¾ in (19 mm)

Beechwood dowel

	1	12 in (300 mm)	½-in (12-mm) diameter

Bore the holes for the dowels ½ in (12 mm) in diameter.

6) Saw the dowels to finish a little longer than required. Cover the surface of your bench with paper to protect it from glue. Glue the dowels and tap them into the holes with a hammer.

7) When the glue has set, trim the dowels flush with the surface of the work with a sharp, finely set smoothing plane. Use the same plane to clean up the outside edges of the shooting board.

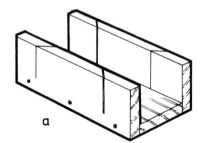

MITER BOX

You could buy a miter box from your tool dealer, but I have simplified the construction so you will find it is easy to make. The miter box (fig. 72) is used to support your wood when cutting a miter. It is commonly used by people who are picture framing.

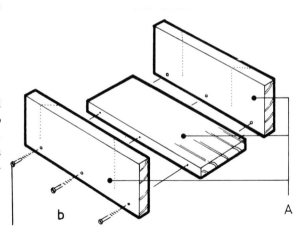

Fig. 72 *The miter box: (a) completed, (b) an exploded view of the construction.*

CONSTRUCTION

1) No allowance has been made in the cutting list for trimming to length because the size of the miter box can be varied. However, avoid making a miter box that is too broad for your backsaw.

2) Trim the ends of the wood square on the shooting board, and make certain that all three pieces are of the same length.

3) Mark out the screw positions on the side pieces with a pencil. Drill the holes ³⁄₁₆ in (5 mm) in diameter through the side pieces. Countersink the holes for the screws.

4) Align each side piece over the base, and gently tap the screws with a hammer so that the screw po-

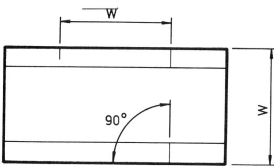

Fig. 73 With a sharp pencil mark out the positions for the saw cuts.

sitions are transferred onto the base. Drill pilot holes in the base piece for the screws with a $\frac{3}{32}$-in (2.5-mm) diameter drill.

5) Glue the sides onto the base, and tighten the screws with a screwdriver. The screws will act as clamps, holding the work together until the glue has set.

6) With a sharp pencil mark out the positions for the saw cuts (fig. 73). The marking-out is done by a) squaring a line across the top of the box b) measuring the width of the box, and transferring this distance from the mark on the side, and c) joining up the marks. The line you draw at c) will cross the box at 45°.

7) Reinforce the pencil lines with knife lines. Carefully cut on the lines with a backsaw. Note that not only must you keep the saw along the 45° lines, but you must also hold the saw perfectly upright.

The marking-out and cutting must be accurate. You will then be able to cut an accurate miter straight from the saw with the miter box without any further trimming being necessary.

8) The miter box will last longer if a length of scrap wood is placed in the bottom of the box. The saw will then cut into the scrap wood rather than into the base of the box.

CUTTING LIST FOR MITER BOX—planed, finished sizes

Hardwood

key	description	quantity	length	width	thickness
A	body	3	9 in (230 mm)	3 in (76 mm)	¾ in (19 mm)

Hardware

6 steel flathead screws   1½ in (38 mm)
                          × no. 8

Things to Make

TOY VAN

This toy van is made chiefly of pinewood and plywood, but the wheels are made of blockboard and the axles are made of beechwood dowel rod. The door of the container is hinged along its top edge; it can be opened by pulling upwards on a small leather strap. The door is kept closed by a magnetic catch. The wood can be finished with several coats of Danish oil, or it can be varnished. This van makes an attractive push-along toy that should delight any child.

The original toy van was made from different pieces of wood that were found in my workshop, so the sizes of the original toy came from the material I had at hand. You need not work to the sizes I have given here. Indeed, you will probably want to design and make other toy vehicles that work on similar principles. A fire engine, tow truck, bus, and racing car are just a few toys you could make.

CONSTRUCTION

1) Square up the ends of the cab by planing in from the edges towards the center with a smoothing plane. Mark out the shaping with a pencil (fig. 74).

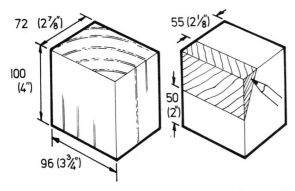

Fig. 74 Mark out the shaping on the cab with a pencil.

2) Hold the cab in the vise, and cut off the waste within ⅛ in (3 mm) of the line with a backsaw. Complete the shaping with a smoothing plane. Round off all sharp corners.

3) Glue the cab onto one end of the plywood engine base. On the original van, after the glue had dried, two dowels—not specified in the cutting list—were inserted through the plywood and into the cab to reinforce this join.

4) Glue one block onto the other end of the plywood engine base. The two fuel tanks can be glued onto the engine base in between the block and the cab.

5) Use the large flathead screw to connect the plywood container base onto the center of the block. Make certain that the container base is free to swivel behind the cab.

6) Glue the second block onto the underside of the container base, allowing a ¾-in (19-mm) space between the block and the end of the base. Glue the plywood packing piece underneath the block.

7) Glue and brad (panel pin) together the sides, the top, and the bottom of the container. Plane the two pieces for the container ends until they are an exact fit inside the container.

Glue and brad (panel pin) one container end inside the container. The other container end can be hinged along the top edge onto the container. A magnetic catch fitted at the bottom edge of the container end will keep this "door" closed. A small leather tab makes a safe and convenient opening device.

Fix the container onto the plywood container base by using four roundheaded screws inserted upwards. Make sure the screws are positioned so their heads will not foul the wheels.

8) Here is the sequence of operations for making the wheels:

a) Take the blockboard pieces for the wheels, and draw in the diagonals with a pencil.

b) With a compass that is set to radius $1\frac{5}{16}$ in (33 mm) draw in the shape of the wheels.

c) Hold the wood in the vise and bore a $\frac{3}{8}$-in (9-mm) diameter hole through the center of each wheel. It is essential that you bore squarely into the wood or the wheels are going to wobble. Bore through the wood until the point of the bit emerges. Turn the wood around so that you can bore a clean hole from the other side.

d) Cut out the wheels by sawing just outside the line with a coping saw. If you find that this tears the wood, clamp a piece of scrap plywood behind your work so the torn edges appear on the scrap wood instead of on your work.

e) You can now clean up the edges of the wheels using abrasive paper, or you can try what I did, and that was to use a disc sander.

A disc sander is a circular metal plate that screws onto the spindle of a radial arm saw, an electric drill, or a lathe. A disc of garnet paper is glued onto the plate, and then, of course, the plate is made to spin at speeds of up to 3,000 rpm. The disc sander is a very dusty machine, and I have found that where the speed of the machine can be varied it is better to run the machine at a slow speed—say 900 rpm—because this reduces the amount of dust that gets into the atmosphere. The garnet paper cuts quickly, but it leaves circular marks that look un-

---

CUTTING LIST FOR TOY VAN (fig. 75)—planed, finished sizes

Softwood or hardwood

key	description	quantity	length	width	thickness
A	cab	1	4 in (100 mm)	3¾ in (96 mm)	2⅞ in (72 mm)
B	fuel tanks	2	1¾ in (45 mm)	1 in (25 mm)	½ in (12 mm)
C	blocks	2	3¾ in (96 mm)	2⅝ in (67 mm)	1 in (25 mm)
D	container sides	2	11 in (280 mm)	4¾ in (120 mm)	⅝ in (15 mm)
E	container top & bottom	2	11 in (280 mm)	5⅜ in (136 mm)	⅜ in (9 mm)
F	container ends	2	4⅛ in (105 mm)	4¾ in (120 mm)	⅝ in (15 mm)
G	axle supports	3	4 in (100 mm)	1⅜ in (35 mm)	¾ in (19 mm)

Plywood

key	description	quantity	length	width	thickness
H	engine base	1	7¾ in (195 mm)	3¾ in (96 mm)	¼ in (6 mm)
I	container base	1	11 in (280 mm)	5⅜ in (136 mm)	¼ in (6 mm)
	packing	1	3¾ in (96 mm)	2⅝ in (67 mm)	¼ in (6 mm)

Blockboard

key	description	quantity	length	width	thickness
J	wheels	6	2¾ in (70 mm)	2¾ in (70 mm)	¾ in (19 mm)

Dowel rod

key	description	quantity	length	width	thickness
K	axles	3	5½ in (140 mm)	⅜-in (9-mm) diameter	

Hardware

4 roundhead screws 1 in (25 mm) × no. 6
1 flathead screw 1¼ in (32 mm) × no. 10
1 piano hinge 4 in (100 mm) long
1 small magnetic catch

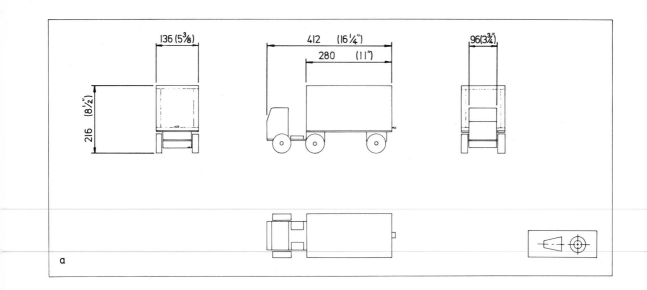

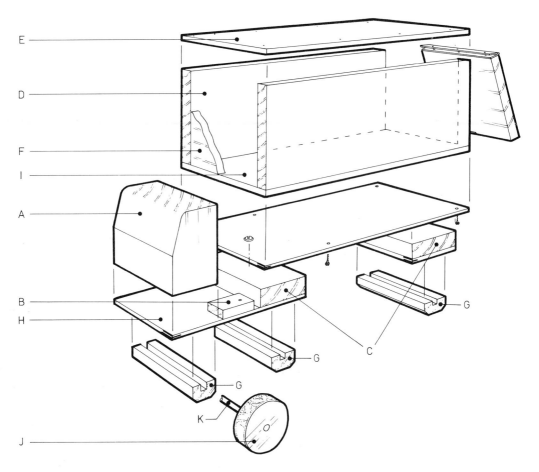

Fig. 75 Toy van: (a) orthographic projection, (b) an exploded view of the construction.

sightly on polished work unless further rubbing down is done by hand.

The wheels can be trimmed on the disc sander by clamping a waste piece of wood onto the sanding table. There must be a ⅜-in (9-mm) diameter hole pre-drilled through the waste piece to allow a dowel to pass through the center of one wheel into the waste piece. The wheel is then slowly, but firmly, rotated by hand while the disc revolves under power.

9) Make a groove that is at least ⅜ in (9 mm) × ⅜ in (9 mm) through the middle of the axle blocks. This groove must be a loose fit on the dowel rod because the dowel rod is to form the axles of the van.

Saw the axles to length and glue them onto the wheels. Rub each axle and the inside of each wheel with a candle—this candle grease will act as a lubricant.

10) Fix the axle blocks to the bottom of the van using contact adhesive—no nails or screws are required here. Then polish or paint the van as you see fit.

TOY TRACTOR

The toy tractor (fig. 76) is built along similar lines to the toy van (and for this reason no construction is given). The tractor, however, is made to a smaller scale than the van.

CUTTING LIST FOR TOY TRACTOR—planed, finished sizes

Softwood or hardwood

key	description	quantity	length	width	thickness
A	cab	1	3⅛ in (80 mm)	2⅞ in (73 mm)	2¼ in (57 mm)
B	engine	1	2⅞ in (73 mm)	1½ in (40 mm)	1½ in (40 mm)
C	axle support	1	1¹¹⁄₁₆ in (44 mm)	1⅝ in (42 mm)	½ in (12 mm)

Plywood

key	description	quantity	length	width	thickness
D	base	1	6 in (152 mm)	2¼ in (57 mm)	¼ in (6 mm)

Blockboard

key	description	quantity	length	width	thickness
E	wheels	2	2⅝ in (67 mm)	2⅝ in (67 mm)	¾ in (19 mm)
E	wheels	2	1⁹⁄₁₆ in (40 mm)	1⁹⁄₁₆ in (40 mm)	¾ in (19 mm)

Dowel rod

key	description	quantity	length	width	thickness
F	axle	1	3¹³⁄₁₆ in (97 mm)	⅜-in (9-mm) diameter	
F	axle	1	3¼ in (82 mm)	¼-in (6-mm) diameter	
G	exhaust	1	2 in (50 mm)	¼-in (6-mm) diameter	

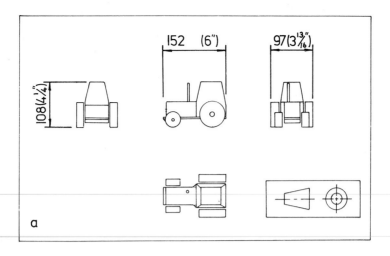

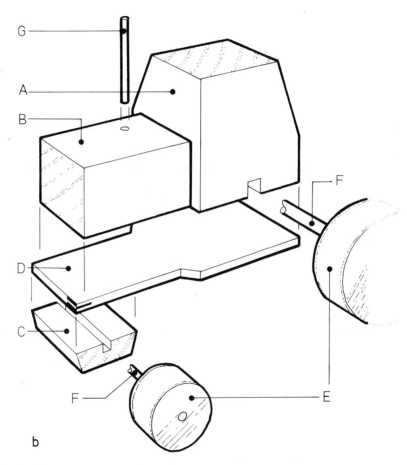

Fig. 76 Toy tractor: (a) orthographic projection, (b) an exploded view of the construction.

PLAYHOUSE

This playhouse (fig. 77) is made from six fibreboard (hardboard) panels. Each panel is made rigid by a partial framing of softwood. The panels are quickly fastened together with eight cabin hooks and two leather straps. The roof panels slot over tabs on the end walls; an interesting feature here is the way one tab has been extended to form a chimney effect. When it is not required, the playhouse can be quickly dismantled and the parts can be stacked flat against a wall.

On the original playhouse the fibreboard (hardboard) panels were painted with white emulsion paint. The panels were then left for the children to decorate with soft-tipped pens and colored paper cutouts.

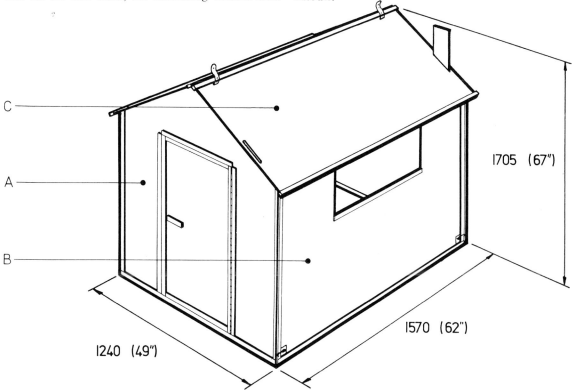

C
A
B

1705 (67")
1570 (62")
1240 (49")

Fig. 77 An assembled playhouse.

CONSTRUCTION

1) Mark out the shapes on the ends and walls with a pencil (fig. 78). Cut out the shapes with either a handsaw or a backsaw. Take particular care with the door opening, as the piece you cut out will be required to make the door. This shaped piece is also rather flimsy, so take particular care not to break it at this stage.

2) All the pieces of softwood of cross-sectional size 7/8 in (21 mm) × 5/8 in (15 mm) must now be grooved with a 1/8-in (3-mm) × 3/8-in (9-mm) deep groove to take the fibreboard. Round off the sharp corners with abrasive paper (fig. 79).

3) Glue the softwood edging strips onto all the pieces of fibreboard where shown (*see* fig. 78).

4) Dowel the edges of the walls near the top and bottom, and drill blind holes on the ends to locate with these dowels (fig. 80).

5) Assemble the ends and walls, using cabin hooks to hold the frames together (*see* fig. 80).

6) Mark out the slots on the roof panels where indicated (fig. 78), but check carefully that these line up with your work so far. A radial arm saw makes easy work of cutting the slots, but it could be done with a knife, file, or narrow chisel.

7) A sliding bolt will hold the door shut (fig. 81).

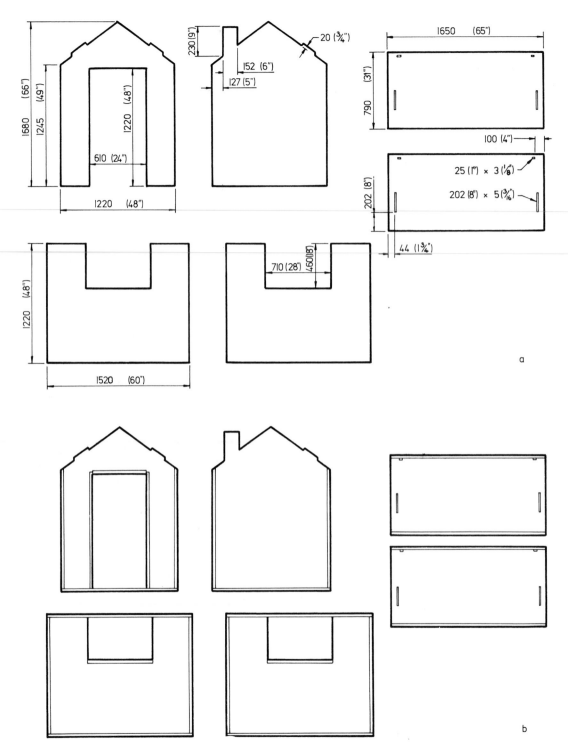

Fig. 78 Playhouse: (a) the shapes of the panels, (b) the panels after the softwood edging strips have been attached.

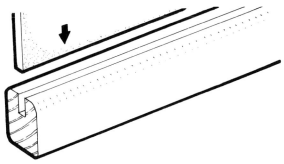

Fig. 79 The softwood edging strips are grooved to take the fibreboard (hardboard) panels.

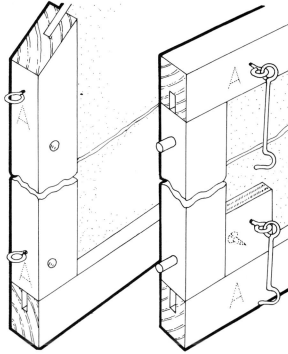

Fig. 80 Dowel the edges of the walls near the top and bottom, and drill "blind" holes in the ends to locate with the dowels.

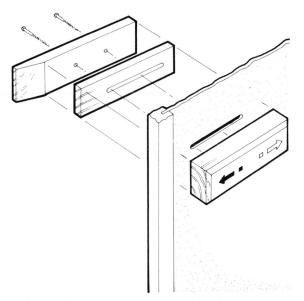

Fig. 81 A wooden sliding bolt will hold the door shut.

CUTTING LIST FOR PLAYHOUSE—planed, finished sizes

Fibreboard (hardboard)

key	description	quantity	length	width	thickness
A	ends	2	66 in (1,680 mm)	48 in (1,220 mm)	⅛ in (3 mm)
B	walls	2	60 in (1,520 mm)	48 in (1,220 mm)	⅛ in (3 mm)
C	roof	2	65 in (1,650 mm)	31 in (790 mm)	⅛ in (3 mm)

Softwood

		quantity	length	width	thickness
		16	50 in (1,270 mm)	⅞ in (21 mm)	⅝ in (15 mm)
		4	62 in (1,580 mm)	⅞ in (21 mm)	⅝ in (15 mm)
		5	66 in (1,680 mm)	⅞ in (21 mm)	⅝ in (15 mm)
		1	17 in (430 mm)	1½ in (40 mm)	½ in (12 mm)
		1	8 in (200 mm)	1½ in (40 mm)	1 in (25 mm)

Plywood

		quantity	length	width	thickness
		4	3 in (76 mm)	1½ in (40 mm)	⅜ in (9 mm)

Dowel

		quantity	length	width
		1	12 in (300 mm)	¼-in (6-mm) diameter

Hardware

1 piano hinge 48 in (1,220 mm) long
8 cabin hooks 1½ in (40 mm)
2 leather straps with buckles, 7 in (180 mm) long—try a cycle shop or use book straps
2 roundhead screws 1¾ in (45 mm) × no. 8
4 flathead screws ½ in (12 mm) × no. 8

PICTURE FRAMING

Picture framing is an interesting and useful task, and can become quite intricate.

The following is a simple and effective method of framing. You should work in this order: 1) decide upon the overall size of the frame, 2) cut the miters, 3) glue the joints, and 4) fit the glass. If you try to work in the reverse order (that is, buy the glass and build the frame around the glass), you will find picture framing much more difficult to do.

With this work it is advisable to buy the picture frame moulding ready-made. The moulding is usually obtainable from art shops, and sometimes picture-framing shops are willing to supply it.

1) Decide upon the overall size for the frame, and saw the frame moulding accurately to length.

2) Cut the miters on the ends of the frame moulding (fig. 82).

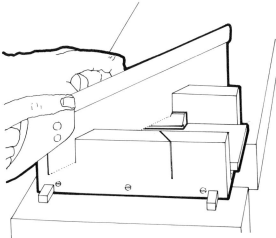

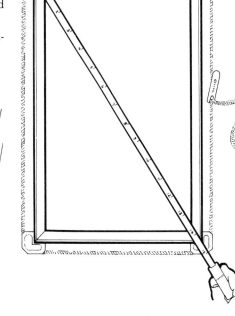

Fig. 82 Saw the miters on the ends of the frame moulding.

Fig. 83 Check the diagonals with a ruler and wipe off surplus glue.

3) Sandpaper (glasspaper) the frame. Brush on one coat of polish, and when dry, rub on a coat of wax.

4) Glue the joints with PVA glue. A string clamp such as the Stanley picture frame vise (Stanley frame cramp) holds the frame together while the glue sets. Check the diagonals with a ruler (fig. 83), and wipe off the surplus glue before setting takes place.

5) The mitered corners can be further strengthened by inserting two brads (panel pins) in each corner, but pre-drill the holes for the brads to avoid splitting the wood (fig. 84).

When the holes have been drilled, hold the frame in the vise and tap in the brads with a hammer. Punch the heads of the brads just below the surface of the wood and cover the head of each brad either with solid beeswax, which you press into the hole with a bradawl, or with plastic wood of the right shade. Next, sandpaper and polish the outside of the frame.

6) Measure the frame for the piece of glass, and buy the glass cut to the size that you require.

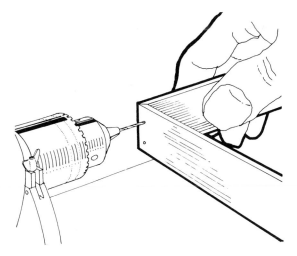

Fig. 84 Pre-drill holes for the brads (panel pins) to avoid splitting the wood.

7) Prepare a backing board the same size as the glass. A piece of corrugated cardboard makes a suitable backing, or an art shop can supply you with a colored backing.

8) Clean the glass with methylated alcohol. Then put the glass in the frame, the picture on the glass, and the backing board on top of the picture (fig. 85). If the picture is much smaller than the backing board you will have to fix it to the backing board with two dabs of adhesive.

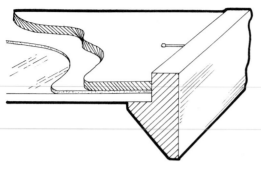

Fig. 85 Put the glass in the frame, the picture on the glass, and then the backing board on top of the picture.

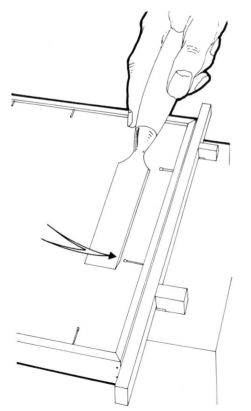

Fig. 86 The brads (panel pins) can be inserted by using the edge of a large firmer chisel as a hammer.

9) Fix the backing board into the frame with ¾-in (19-mm) brads. The brads need to be spaced at about 4-in (100-mm) intervals. The brads can be inserted by using the edge of a large firmer chisel as though it were a hammer (fig. 86).

10) Seal the backing board into the frame, using 2-in-(50-mm) wide brown-paper tape over the gap between the backing board and frame.

11) Insert two small screw eyes one-third the way down from the top of the frame. String the frame with either nylon cord or picture wire.

TABLE LAMPS

Here are three different table lamps that can be made with pieces of wood left over from larger constructions. Apart from using scrap pieces of wood, other materials such as leather, vinyl, or fabric can be included in the design. Each lamp uses a brass tube to support the socket (bulb holder) and the shade; these tubes are available from almost any good electrical store. All the lamps use metal sockets (bulb holders) so that the brass tubes are properly grounded (earthed).

You may like to copy one of these designs, but I hope you may prefer to be more creative. Using your own imagination and skill, you can construct a table lamp from the scrap pieces of wood in your workshop.

Design one (fig. 87):

This lamp has fourteen uprights, and the shape is based upon that of Liverpool Cathedral. The method employed is similar to that used for balsa-wood model aircraft, with the parts slotted and glued together. The original lamp was made from mahogany and teak.

CONSTRUCTION

1) Use a pencil compass to mark out the top disc and bottom disc with 6-in (150-mm) and 7½-in (190-mm) diameter circles respectively. Cut to shape with a coping saw, and trim the edges with a spokeshave. Drill a hole through the center of each disc to take the metal column.

2) Mark out and cut the fourteen slots ⅛ in (3 mm) wide to receive the uprights. The slots on the original

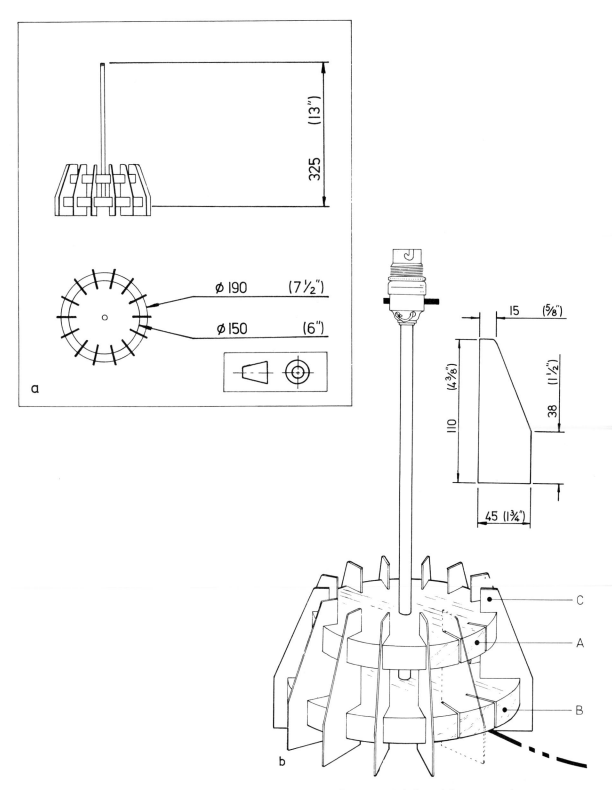

Fig. 87 Table lamp, design one: (a) orthographic projection, (b) a pictorial view of the construction.

CUTTING LIST FOR TABLE LAMP (DESIGN ONE)—planed, finished sizes

Hardwood

key	description	quantity	length	width	thickness
A	top disc	1	6 in (150 mm)	6 in (150 mm)	¾ in (19 mm)
B	bottom disc	1	7½ in (190 mm)	7½ in (190 mm)	¾ in (19 mm)
C	uprights	14	4⅜ in (110 mm)	1¾ in (45 mm)	⅛ in (3 mm)

column were cut on both discs at the same time using a machine bandsaw.

3) Shape the profile of the uprights.

4) Clean up the uprights and the surfaces of two discs using abrasive paper.

5) Glue the uprights in position. Take care to remove the surplus glue so that you make a neat job.

6) Polish the lamp.

7) Fit the metal column through the centers of both discs, and glue the column in position with epoxy resin adhesive. The column should finish flush with the lower surface of the bottom disc.

8) Fit the electric cord.

Design two (fig. 88):

This design consists of two hardwood discs. The top disc is thicker than the bottom disc because it has to support the brass tube. A chipboard disc, which is marginally smaller in diameter than the other two discs, and which has a ⅜-in (9-mm) wide slot cut in it from the circumference to the center, is placed in between the two hardwood discs. Four wood screws inserted from underneath the bottom

disc hold the construction together. The purpose of the chipboard, which is heavy, is to make the design stable. The edge of the chipboard can be concealed by a strip of leather, vinyl, or fabric. The original lamp was made from mahogany and was trimmed with brown vinyl.

CONSTRUCTION

1) Use a pencil compass to mark out the top and bottom discs with 8¼-in (210-mm) diameter circles. Mark out the middle disc with a 7¾-in (197-mm) diameter circle.

2) Cut the discs to shape with a coping saw, then trim the edges with a spokeshave.

3) Mark out and cut the ⅜-in (9-mm)-wide slot for the cord from the edge to the center of the chipboard disc.

4) Drill a hole through the center of the top disc to receive the brass column.

5) Drill holes for the screws through the bottom disc, the middle disc, and into the top disc. Counter-

CUTTING LIST FOR TABLE LAMP (DESIGN TWO)—planed, finished sizes

Hardwood

key	description	quantity	length	width	thickness
A	top disc	1	8¼ in (210 mm)	8¼ in (210 mm)	1⅛ in (28 mm)
B	bottom disc	1	8¼ in (210 mm)	8¼ in (210 mm)	½ in (12 mm)

Chipboard

key	description	quantity	length	width	thickness
C	middle disc	1	7¾ in (197 mm)	7¾ in (197 mm)	⅝ in (16 mm)

Hardware

4 brass flathead screws 1¾ in (45 mm) × no. 10

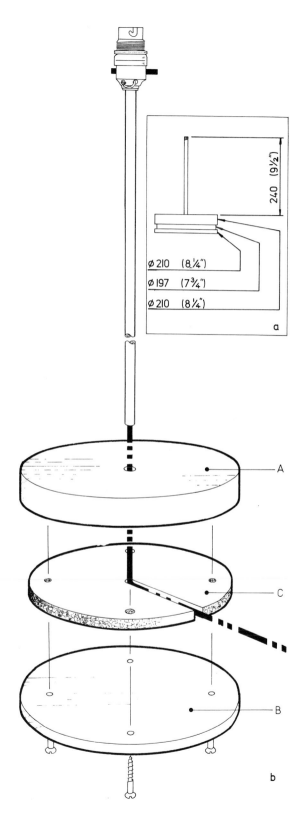

Ø 210 (8¼")

Ø 197 (7¾")

Ø 210 (8¼")

240 (9½")

a

A

C

B

b

Fig. 88 Table lamp, design two: (a) elevation, (b) an exploded view of the construction.

sink the holes in the underside of the bottom disc.

6) Cut a strip of leather, vinyl, or fabric for the edge of the middle disc. Glue this in position and tuck the ends of the strip inside the slot.

7) Polish the exterior surfaces of the hardwood parts. Glue the brass column into the hole in the top disc, using epoxy resin adhesive.

8) Fit the electric cord.

9) Screw the discs together.

10) Sticky-back baize can be used to cover the underside of the bottom disc.

Design three (fig. 89):

This lamp is built like a box that is stood on end. Two shaped plywood panels are used to cover the open sides, and these panels are decorated with thin leather skins. The top of the lamp is made from slightly thicker wood than the sides and bottom because the top has to support the brass tube which passes through its center. The top is also curved to make the lamp more interesting.

The plywood side panels can be glued into position, or one panel can be glued and the other fitted with two magnetic catches. The latter makes the task of fitting the cord more simple because it means that you can get your hands inside. It also means that you have a convenient hiding place!

If you decide that this lamp is too tall you could reduce it by as much as two-thirds of its height.

The original lamp was made from muninga, and the panels were covered with brown suede leather.

CONSTRUCTION

1) Mark out and cut the top and bottom pieces 5⅛ in (130 mm) long. Square the ends of each piece.

2) Mark out and cut the sides 12 in (300 mm) long. Square the ends of these pieces.

3) Glue the ends of the top and bottom pieces, and press them against the side pieces. Use clamps to hold this box-like construction together. Check that the box is square by measuring the diagonals, and check that it is flat by sighting across the sides. Carefully bend the box until all is correct. Wipe off the surplus glue with a damp rag, and leave the box in clamps overnight for the glue to dry.

4) Carefully clean up the box with a smoothing plane, and level the joints at the corners. Mark out a gentle curve on the top piece by asking someone else to slightly bend a steel ruler while you draw around it with a pencil. Shape the top with a spokeshave.

5) Plane the edges of the rabbet panels until the panels just fit inside the box.

6) Position each side panel in turn against the box, and transfer the internal size of the box onto the panel with a pencil.

7) Glue the rabbet panels onto the side panels, taking care that the rabbet panels are positioned within the pencil guidelines.

8) Mark out and cut the profile shape on each side panel. Round over the long edges and the top edge of each side panel with either a rasp or a plane.

9) Glue the leather or fabric onto the side panels. The covering material must be wrapped around the edges and slightly onto the back of the side panels.

10) Drill the hole in the center of the top for the brass tube. Glue the tube into the hole with epoxy resin adhesive.

11) Drill a small hole through the side of the box near the bottom for the cord.

CUTTING LIST FOR TABLE LAMP (DESIGN THREE)—planed, finished sizes

Hardwood

key	description	quantity	length	width	thickness
A	sides	2	12 in (300 mm)	4⅜ in (110 mm)	⅞ in (22 mm)
B	bottom	1	5½ in (140 mm)	4⅜ in (110 mm)	⅞ in (22 mm)
C	top	1	5½ in (140 mm)	4⅜ in (110 mm)	1 in (25 mm)

Plywood

key	description	quantity	length	width	thickness
D	side panels	2	11⅝ in (295 mm)	7 in (180 mm)	⅜ in (9 mm)
E	rabbet panels	2	10¼ in (260 mm)	5¼ in (133 mm)	⅜ in (9 mm)

12) Polish the hardwood.

13) Fit the cord.

14) Glue the side panels in position, or glue one panel and use two magnetic catches to retain the other panel.

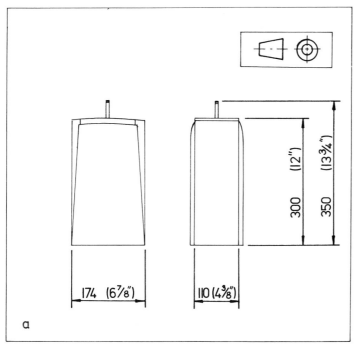

a

Fig. 89 Table lamp, design three: (a) orthographic projection, (b) an exploded view of the construction.

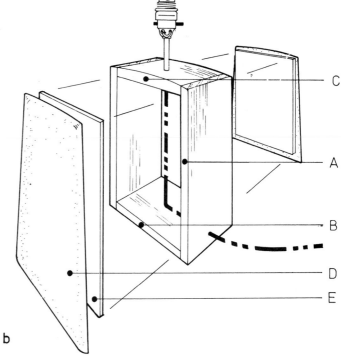

b

BRIEFCASE

This briefcase has been designed to carry legal (metric A4-)-sized sheets of paper—the internal measurements are 14 in (355 mm) × 9¾ (245 mm). By altering the measurements, you could adapt the case for other uses, such as carrying books, writing materials and camera equipment. The case is chiefly made from plywood, and the fittings—hinges, catches, handle—are easily obtainable from shops that deal in leather goods. The outside of the case can be covered in either vinyl or leather, and the inside of the case can be lined with baize.

CONSTRUCTION

1) Trim the front and back pieces to 14½ in (370 mm) in length.
2) Trim the end pieces to 11 in (280 mm) in length.
3) It is optional whether you mark out and cut the rabbet joint on the end pieces. The purpose of the joint is to strengthen the corners of the briefcase.

4) Glue and brad (panel pin) the corners together. Check that the frame is square by measuring the diagonals, and check that the frame is flat by sighting across the ends. Carefully bend the frame until it is correct. Wipe off surplus glue with a damp rag, then leave the frame overnight for the glue to dry.
5) When the glue has set, make sure that the top and bottom edges of the frame are level at the corners. Plane off any discrepancy.
6) Glue the plywood top and bottom onto the frame. Weight the assembly to hold the parts tightly together until the glue has set.
7) Clean up the outside of the case with a smoothing plane, but take care not to touch the plane blade on any of the brads (panel pins). Slightly round the plywood top and bottom where they meet the sides (fig. 91).
8) Use a mortise gauge to gauge two parallel lines around the case. The lines mark the division between the lid and the base. These lines must be ⅛ in (3 mm) apart.
9) Use a backsaw to cut around the case to separate the lid from the base.

CUTTING LIST FOR BRIEFCASE (fig. 90)—finished sizes

Plywood

key	description	quantity	length	width	thickness
A	front & back	2	15 in (380 mm)	3 in (76 mm)	⅜ in (9 mm)
B	ends	2	11½ in (290 mm)	3 in (76 mm)	⅜ in (9 mm)
C	top & bottom	2	15½ in (395 mm)	11 in (280 mm)	⅛ in (3 mm)

Vinyl or leather

| | covering | 2 | 22 in (560 mm) | 17½ in (445 mm) | |

Sticky-back baize

| | lining | 2 | 22 in (560 mm) | 17½ in (445 mm) | |

Hardware

2 briefcase hinges with built-in stay
2 briefcase catches
1 handle
Chromium-plated roundhead screws to fit the above
4 studs—aluminium football boot studs will do

10) Carefully clean up the sawn edges with a smoothing plane.

11) Glue the base and the sides of the case well. Stand the base centrally on the back of one of the pieces of vinyl. Cut the vinyl and bring up the end piece, and then the front piece (fig. 92). Miter the vinyl on the top edge (fig. 93). Stick the vinyl on the edge and just inside the base.

12) Repeat for the lid.

13) Cut one piece of sticky-back baize to fit the in-side of the base. Stick this in position.

Cut four pieces of cardboard to fit inside the edges of the base. Cover these pieces with sticky-back baize, allowing the baize to wrap over the edges and onto the back of each piece of cardboard. Glue these pieces into the base.

14) Repeat for the lid.

15) Screw on the hinges, the catches, the handle, and the studs.

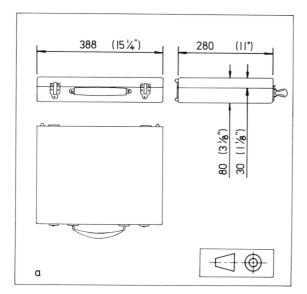

a

Fig. 91 Slightly round the top and bottom of the plywood where they meet the sides.

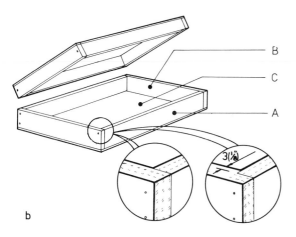

b

Fig. 90 Briefcase: (a) orthographic projection, (b) an exploded view of the construction.

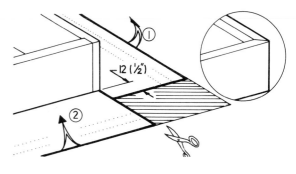

Fig. 92 Cut the vinyl at the corner, and then bring up the end piece and the front piece.

Fig. 93 (inset) Miter the vinyl on the top corner.

93

KITCHEN CUPBOARD

This compact kitchen cupboard is suitable for use in a small home. The design included here illustrates many of the ways in which melamine-faced chipboard can be used.

At a (fig. 94), there is a cupboard that is posi-tioned high up against a ceiling. The two doors are hinged on piano hinges. A long aluminium finger pull is attached to the bottom edge of each door. The doors are held in the open position by automatic stays, and are kept in the closed position by magnetic catches.

At b (fig. 94), there is a large cupboard that is

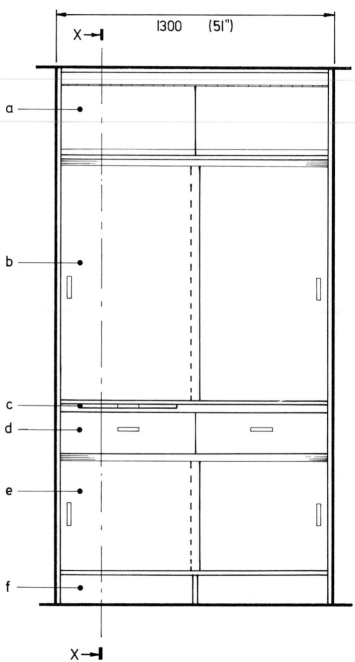

Fig. 94a Kitchen cupboard: orthographic projection.

concealed by a pair of sliding doors. Inside the cupboard there are three shelves that are adjustable in height.

At c (fig. 94), there is a small shelf that can be pulled out to form a ledge. This makes a handy place for resting coffee cups or a mixing bowl.

At d (fig. 94), there are two drawers.

At e (fig. 94), there is another cupboard. This is smaller than the first cupboard, and it contains just one shelf that is adjustable in height. This cupboard is also concealed by a pair of sliding doors.

At f (fig. 94), there is a toe space that is used also for storing shoes. It is easy to be unconcerned about the idea of shoe storage space, but in the smaller home where space is at a premium such an idea can make a big difference.

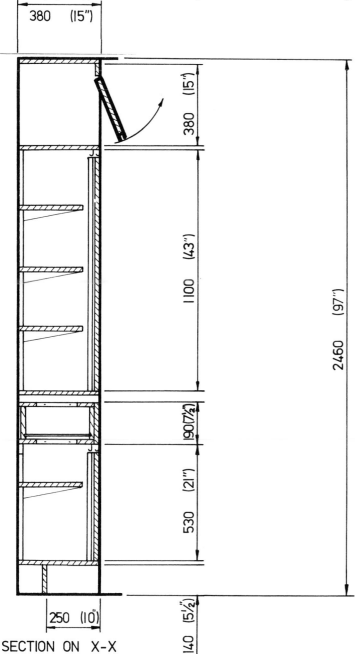

380　(15")

380　(15")

1100　(43")

2460　(97")

90(7½)

530　(21")

250　(10)

140　(5½)

SECTION ON X-X

Fig. 94b Kitchen cupboard: side view of cabinet.

CUTTING LIST FOR KITCHEN CUPBOARD (figs. 95 & 96)—finished sizes

Melamine-faced chipboard ⅝ in (15 mm) thick

key	description	quantity	length	width	thickness
A	sides	2	97 in (2,460 mm)	15 in (380 mm)	
B	fixed shelves	4	49¾ in (1,264 mm)	15 in (380 mm)	
C	top rail	1	49¾ in (1,264 mm)	2 in (50 mm)	
D	adjustable shelves	4	49⅝ in (1,260 mm)	12 in (300 mm)	
E	shoe rabbet	1	49¾ in (1,264 mm)	5½ in (140 mm)	
E	shoe rabbet	1	10 in (250 mm)	5½ in (140 mm)	
F	tray	1	22 in (560 mm)	14½ in (370 mm)	
G	framing	2	49¾ in (1,264 mm)	2 in (50 mm)	
G	framing	2	13¾ in (350 mm)	2 in (50 mm)	
L	drawer fronts	2	24⅞ in (632 mm)	7½ in (190 mm)	
	top doors	2	24⅞ in (632 mm)	13 in (330 mm)	
	middle doors	2	43 in (1,100 mm)	25¼ in (640 mm)	
	bottom doors	2	21 in (530 mm)	25¼ in (640 mm)	

Hardwood

key	description	quantity	length	width	thickness
H	runners	2	14 in (360 mm)	4 in (100 mm)	1¼ in (32 mm)
H	runners	2	14 in (360 mm)	2 in (50 mm)	¾ in (19 mm)
J	runners	8	10 in (250 mm)	¾ in (19 mm)	¾ in (19 mm)

Softwood

key	description	quantity	length	width	thickness
K	cross pieces	4	49¾ in (1,264 mm)	3 in (76 mm)	¾ in (19 mm)
M	drawer	4	24 in (610 mm)	6 in (150 mm)	⅝ in (16 mm)
N	drawer sides	4	14¼ in (362 mm)	6 in (150 mm)	⅝ in (16 mm)

Blockboard

key	description	quantity	length	width	thickness
I	separators	3	15 in (380 mm)	7½ in (190 mm)	¾ in (19 mm)

Plywood

key	description	quantity	length	width	thickness
O	drawer bottom	2	24 in (610 mm)	14 in (355 mm)	⅛ in (3 mm)

Hardware

22 plastic block joints with chipboard screws
 2 sliding door tracks 49¾ in (1,264 mm) long for bypassing doors
 1 piano hinge 49¾ in (1,264 mm) long
30 wall plugs and screws
¼ lb (100 g) of 1½-in (38-mm) oval nails
 9 drawer handles
 3 pieces of adjustable shelving 43 in (1,100 mm) long
 3 pieces of adjustable shelving 21 in (530 mm) long
12 12-in (300-mm) adjustable shelving brackets

CONSTRUCTION

The concept behind the construction of this kitchen cupboard is that the two cupboards that are fitted with adjustable shelving should have the shelving supports screwed to the wall initially. Then the rest of the cupboard—or box-like structure—is built and attached to the wall independently of the shelving supports. The parts of the cupboard are held together with plastic block joints. As long as you can cut melamine-faced chipboard cleanly, and you can edge the chipboard with iron-on edging strip, there should be no end to your creative achievements.

The sizes of this kitchen cupboard have been given

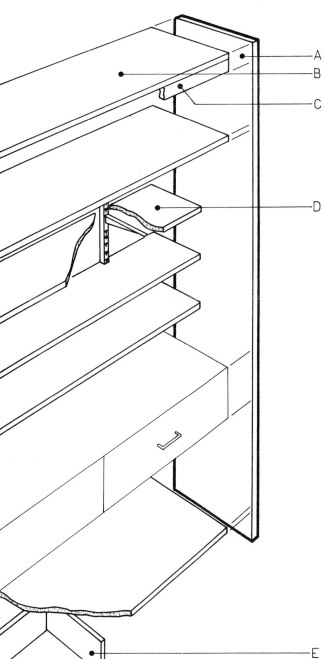

Fig. 95 Kitchen cupboard: exploded view.

so that you can copy them, but there is no reason why you cannot make built-in furniture according to your own design with the methods outlined here. Just remember that chipboard is not a good supporter of loads, so on a shelf length as you see here of 49¾ in (1,264 mm) three shelving brackets are required to prevent the shelf from bending.

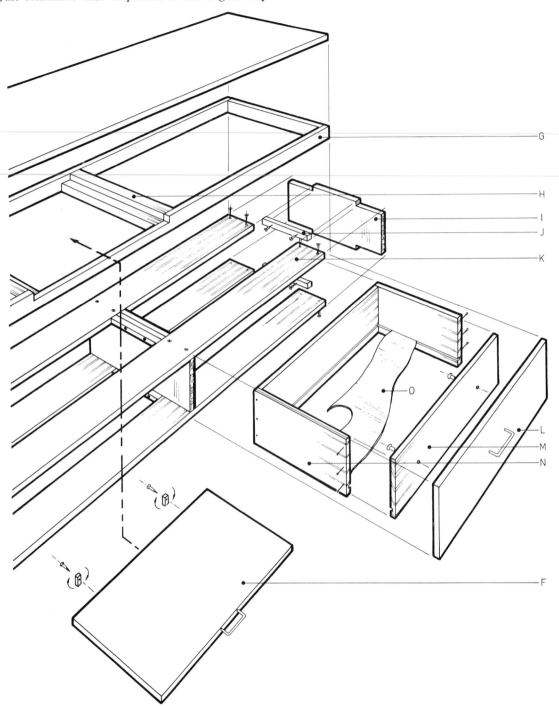

Fig. 96 Kitchen cupboard: An exploded view of the drawer unit.

ADJUSTABLE STANDARD LAMP

CONSTRUCTION

This adjustable standard lamp (fig. 97) uses a lighting unit of the type used for store window displays. The main advantages in using a unit of this type are that the lamps can be raised or lowered, as well as swivelled and tilted; therefore, illumination can be provided exactly where it is required. The standard lamp is fitted with casters to make it fully mobile, and two hooks screwed onto the back of the wooden upright make a convenient place to store the surplus cord.

Considerable effort has been made to achieve a stable result. Although the standard lamp could be constructed with a lighting unit made by another manufacturer, you must realize that increasing the height of the column or shortening the feet could make the standard lamp unstable.

The track of the lighting unit must be grounded (earthed). I am satisfied with the electrical safety of the unit used here. However, the manufacturer has told me that though safe, the track has not been designed to overcome the problem of children with lead soldiers. So keep the lamp away from children, and don't put the hot lamps close to the curtains (drapes).

1) Mark the upright to length with a knife (fig. 98), and square the knife lines around the wood. Then mark out the mortise limit lines on two adjacent surfaces with just a pencil.

2) Hold the pieces for the feet together in a vise, and mark out with a knife (fig. 99).

Remove the wood from the vise, and square the lines around each piece. Saw off the waste from the ends.

3) Set the spurs of the mortise gauge to ⅜ in (9 mm) apart, and set the stock on the gauge to within ⅜ in (9 mm) of the nearest spur. Gauge the tenons on the long feet, and the two mortises at the base of the upright (fig. 100).

4) Chop the mortises 1⅛ in (32 mm) deep. If you do not own a ⅜-in (9-mm) mortise chisel, you will have to make two parallel cuts with the ¼-in (6-mm) chisel. Saw the tenons.

Mark out and cut the secret haunches, and remove the ⅛-in (3-mm) covers from the tenons.

The ends of the tenons will have to be sawn at 45° for the tenons to fit properly inside the upright; take care at this stage because the feet are left- and right-handed and you need to know which is which before you do any cutting.

CUTTING LIST FOR ADJUSTABLE LAMP—planed, finished sizes

Hardwood

key	description	quantity	length	width	thickness
A	upright	1	64 in (1,620 mm)	1½ in (40 mm)	1½ in (40 mm)
B	feet	2	19 in (480 mm)	2¾ in (70 mm)	1½ in (40 mm)

Dowel

key	description	quantity	length	width	thickness
C		1	12 in (300 mm)	¼-in (6-mm) diameter	

Hardware

track 49 in (1,250 mm) long
2 lamps
2 aluminium coat hooks
4 mini-casters, plate or peg fitting

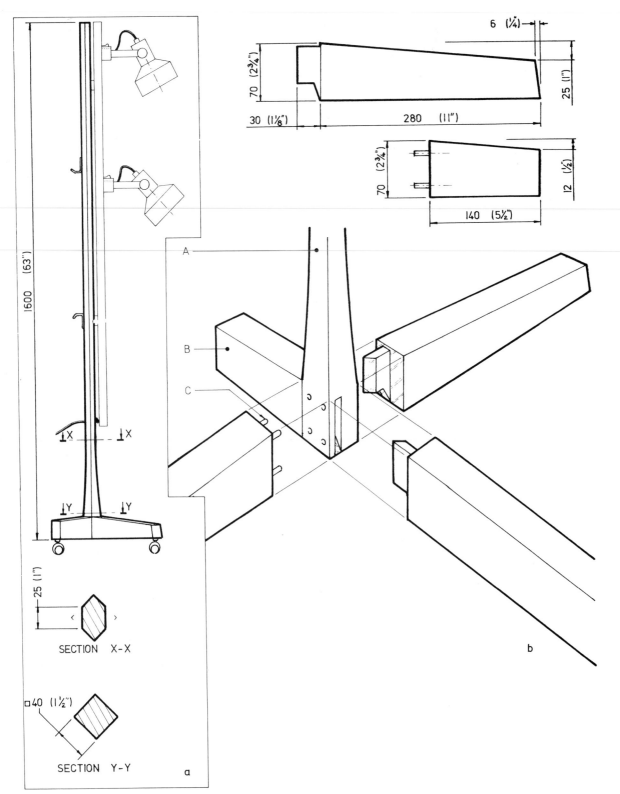

6 (¼")

70 (2¾")

25 (1")

30 (1⅛")   280   (11")

70 (2¾")

12 (½")

140   (5½")

1600   (63")

A

B

C

X   X

Y   Y

25 (1")

SECTION   X-X

□40 (1½")

SECTION   Y-Y

a

b

Fig. 97 Adjustable standard lamp: (a) orthographic projection, (b) an exploded view of the construction.

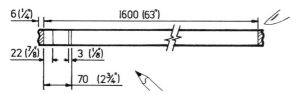

Fig. 98 *Mark the upright to length with a knife and mark the mortise limit lines with a pencil.*

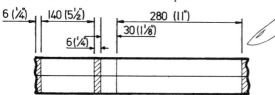

Fig. 99 *Hold the pieces for the feet together, and mark them out with a knife.*

5) Fit the joints together without glue. With the parts together mark out the 1-in (25-mm) chamfers front and back of the column with a pencil. The chamfers disappear just above the feet (fig. 101).

Shape the chamfers with a smoothing plane and spokeshave.

Mark out the shaping for the tops of the feet with a pencil. Shape the tops of the feet with the smoothing plane.

6) Mark out the shaping for the ends of the feet, but do not cut until after the gluing-up stage; otherwise, clamping the work can be very difficult.

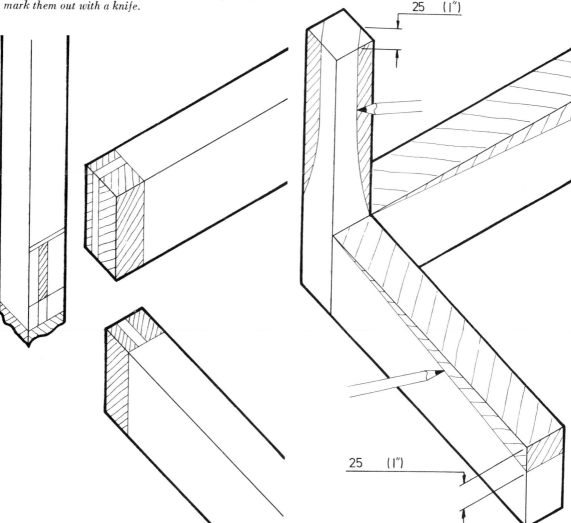

Fig. 100 *Gauge the tenons on the long feet, and gauge the two mortises on the base of the upright.*

Fig. 101 *Mark out the shaping on the column and on the long feet.*

7) Mark out the shaping on the short feet (*see* fig. 97). Shape both of the feet, and prepare them for polishing.

Cut the upright accurately to length, and clean it up ready for polishing.

8) Polish all the surfaces, but avoid getting polish onto surfaces that will be glued.

9) Glue the long feet into the upright. Note that it will be easier to glue the feet one at a time; then clamp and wait for the glue to set before continuing with the second foot. Remove surplus glue with a damp rag before it sets.

10) Use the pin method to locate the positions for four 1½-in (40-mm) × ¼-in (6-mm) dowels in the short feet. Try to position the dowels so that they do not interfere with each other, and do not disturb the existing joints. Drill the holes for these dowels ⅞ in (22 mm) deep.

11) Glue and dowel the short feet in place one foot at a time. Wait for the glue to set on the first before you tackle the second.

12) Screw the track in position on the front of the upright.

13) Two aluminium coat hooks screwed on the back of the upright at 18-in (460-mm) centers make a handy means of winding up the electric cord.

14) Drill a ¼-in (6-mm) diameter hole through the upright to line up with the electrical connections at the end of the track. This hole will take the cord.

15) Wire the lamp with a three-core cord. Tying a knot in the cord on the track side of the upright will prevent the cord from tugging free of the electrical connections.

16) Fix the casters onto the feet.

TILE-TOP TABLE

Here is a table (fig. 102) designed on lines of classical simplicity. This surely is one of the most attractive pieces of furniture described in this book. The tiles may help to remind some readers of a holiday in Italy—a country that is famous for its ceramics.

The original table was made from teak and had tiles of an orange peel color and texture.

CUTTING LIST FOR TILE-TOP TABLE—planed, finished sizes

Hardwood

key	description	quantity	length	width	thickness
A	legs	4	18½ in (470 mm)	1⅜ in (35 mm)	1⅜ in (35 mm)
B	upper rails	4	20 in (510 mm)	2½ in (63 mm)	⅞ in (22 mm)
C	lower rails	4	20 in (510 mm)	1 in (25 mm)	⅞ in (22 mm)
D	strips	4	18 in (460 mm)	1 in (25 mm)	½ in (12 mm)

Chipboard

E	top	1	18½ in (470 mm)	18½ in (470 mm)	½ in (12 mm)

Ceramic border tiles

F	tiles	9	6 in (150 mm)	6 in (150 mm)	3/16 in (5 mm)

Hardware

12 brass flathead screws 1 in (25 mm) × no. 8
8 brass flathead screws 1 in (25 mm) × no. 6

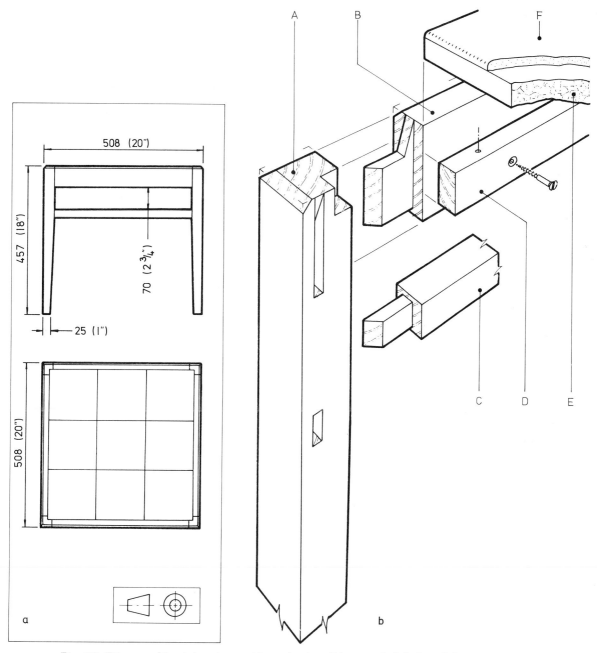

508 (20")

457 (18")

70 (2 3/4")

25 (1")

508 (20")

a

A

B

F

C

D

E

b

Fig. 102 Tile-top table: (a) orthographic projection, (b) an exploded view of the construction.

CONSTRUCTION OF THE TABLE

1) Choose the tiles first because you may have to alter the size of the table to fit the tiles.
2) Lay the tiles on the chipboard. Allow for a small gap between all the tiles and between the tiles and the inside edge of the table. Mark the overall size

on the chipboard, and cut the chipboard to size. The table must now be made to fit the chipboard top.
3) Choose the best surfaces on each piece of wood; these must be seen on the outside of the table, so mark these surfaces in pencil with face-side and face-edge marks.

103

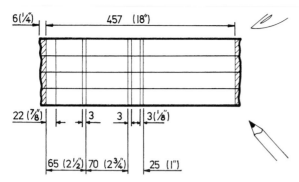

Fig. 103 *Hold the legs together and mark them to length with a knife; mark the mortise positions with a pencil.*

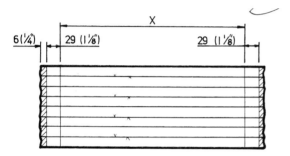

Fig. 104 *Place the eight rails together and mark them to length.*

then set the stock of the gauge so that the spurs will mark centrally along the edge of the rails. Gauge the tenons; then gauge the mortises from the face-sides and the face-edges of the legs. Hatch in the waste (fig. 105).

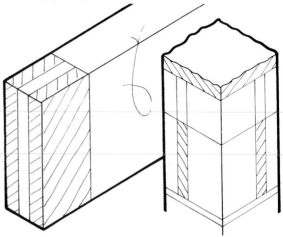

Fig. 105 *Gauge the tenons, then gauge the mortises. Hatch in the waste.*

8) Chop the mortises $1\frac{1}{8}$ in (28 mm) deep. Note that the joint between the legs and the upper rails will be a secret haunched mortise-and-tenon (*see* fig. 44), while the joint for the lower rails is an ordinary mortise-and-tenon (*see* figs. 38–41). Cut the tenons, then remove the haunches and covers.

9) Miter the ends of all the tenons so that there is about a $\frac{1}{8}$-in (3-mm) expansion gap between them inside the legs (fig. 106). Fit the joints together without glue, and number them on the outside A-A, B-B, and so on.

10) When the table is together, but the joints are not glued, mark out in pencil:

a) the taper on the inside of the legs. This starts just below the lower rails and finishes with the foot of each leg 1 in (25 mm) square.

b) the pocket on the inside top of each leg so that the tiles will finish nearly flush with the upper rails (fig. 107).

   Take the table apart to plane the taper on the inside of the legs. Cut the pocket on each leg by partly sawing, then chiselling across the grain with a $1\frac{1}{4}$-in (32-mm) chisel.

11) Clean up all the inside surfaces, and round off all sharp corners where it is possible. Polish the inside surfaces.

4) Place the four legs together face-side downwards. Mark out the overall length with a knife, and mark out the mortise positions with a pencil (fig. 103). Separate the pieces. Square the knife lines around each leg, and hatch in the waste. Square the pencil lines on to one other surface, but that surface must not be the face-side or the face-edge.

5) Place the eight rails together, face-edge upwards, and with a knife mark out the waste at one end the length of one tenon (fig. 104). The rabbet length must be accurately calculated so that the chipboard will fit neatly between the rails. (The distance will probably be about $17\frac{1}{4}$ in [437 mm].) Mark out the length of the tenon at the other end. Hatch in the waste and square the knife lines around each rail.

6) Saw the waste from the ends of the rails.

7) Set the spurs on the mortise gauge to the same distance apart as your $\frac{1}{4}$-in (6-mm) mortise chisel;

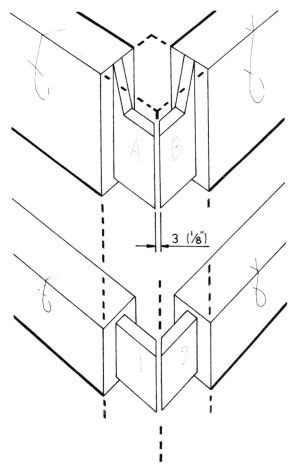

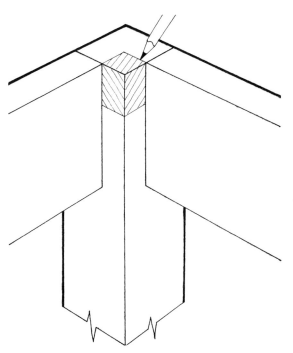

3 (⅛")

Fig. 107 Mark out in pencil the pocket on the top of each leg so that the tiles finish almost flush with the upper rails.

Fig. 106 Miter the ends of the tenons so that there is a small gap between the ends of the tenons when they are inserted into the legs.

12) Glue up two legs, one upper rail and one lower rail. Use bar clamps to hold the frame together while the glue dries. Check that the frame is flat by sighting across it, and check that the frame is square by measuring the diagonals. Carefully bend the frame or move the clamps until all is correct.

Next, glue up the opposing frame.

Finally, when the glue in the frames is dry, the whole table can be glued together. Check that the table is not twisted, and check that the diagonals across the top and the feet are the same.

13) Clean up the outside surfaces. Cut the waste from the feet and from the top of the legs.

14) Mark a chamfer ¼ in (6 mm) × ¼ in (6

mm) around the top with a pencil. Shape the chamfer with a smoothing plane.

15) Clean up the four strips. These are used to support the top. Cut each strip to length so it fits inside the table. Drill, countersink, and fix each strip with three 1-in (25-mm) no. 8 screws.

16) Polish the outside of the table.

17) Drill, countersink, and fix the chipboard top to the strips with eight 1-in (25-mm) no. 6 screws.

FIXING THE TILES

18) Arrange the tiles in a suitable pattern, number the backs of the tiles, and pencil corresponding numbers on the chipboard.

Use a small can of the type of contact adhesive that allows for some adjustment of the work. Spread the adhesive evenly over the backs of the tiles and on the chipboard. Place the tiles in position, using thin pieces of cardboard as spacers. When correct, press the tiles in position and remove the spacers.

19) Fill the spaces between the tiles with plaster

filler. Surplus plaster can be removed with a damp cloth.

FORMICA-TOP TABLE

This plastic laminate-topped table (fig. 108) is a practical addition to any home. Its large, wipe-clean surface makes it useful as a coffee table, a drinks table, or occasionally as a games table. Four slats underneath the top make a convenient place for putting books and magazines.

Plastic laminates are produced in many designs, so choosing one to suit your furnishings should present no difficulty. A marble laminate was chosen for the original table, and this created a "marble"-topped table without the excessive weight of true marble. The framework of the original table was made from mahogany.

CONSTRUCTION OF THE TOP

1) Check that the blockboard measures 28½ in (720 mm) × 17 in (430 mm). Measure the diag-onals to see that all the corners are right angles. Plane off any discrepancy.

2) Clean up the underneath face of the blockboard with abrasive paper, and clean up the edges of the top battens where they will show.

3) Place the top battens in position, and draw with a pencil a glue line on the blockboard in such a way that the line will be concealed when the battens are in place.

4) Glue the top battens to the blockboard with con-tact adhesive (fig. 109).

5) Allow the glue to strengthen overnight, then place the edge of the top square and level with the battens.

6) The laminate top now has to be laid. Be careful when matching patterns, for the pattern on the top should match the pattern on the edges.

Mark out with a pencil 1¾-in (44-mm)-wide strips of laminate for the edges. These strips can be cut from the sheet in one of three ways: using a backsaw at a low angle; using a circular saw; using a bandsaw. If a radial arm saw is used the laminate should be cut from the back. Glue these strips of laminate into position with contact adhesive.

CUTTING LIST FOR FORMICA-TOPPED TABLE—planed, finished sizes

Hardwood

key	description	quantity	length	width	thickness
A	top battens	2	29 in (740 mm)	1½ in (38 mm)	⅞ in (22 mm)
B	legs	4	19½ in (500 mm)	1½ in (38 mm)	1½ in (38 mm)
C	top end rails	2	17 in (430 mm)	1¾ in (45 mm)	1½ in (38 mm)
D	lower end rails	2	17 in (430 mm)	1½ in (38 mm)	1 in (25 mm)
E	slats	4	31 in (790 mm)	1¾ in (45 mm)	¾ in (19 mm)

Blockboard

F	top	1	28½ in (720 mm)	17 in (430 mm)	¾ in (19 mm)

Formica, plastic laminate

G		1	28½ in (720 mm)	22 in (560 mm)	

Dowel

		1	24 in (600 mm)	⅜-in (9-mm) diameter	

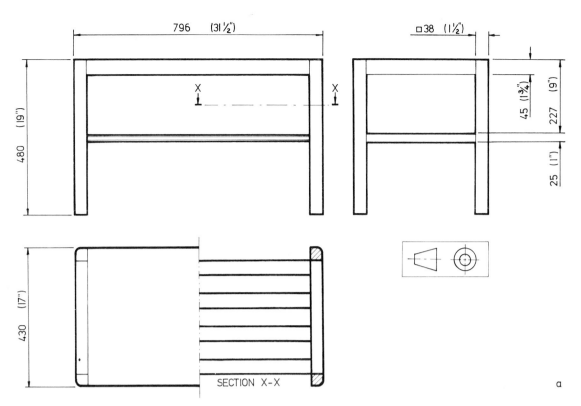

796 (31½")

□38 (1½")

480 (19")

45 (1¾")

227 (9")

25 (1")

X

X

430 (17")

SECTION X-X

a

Fig. 108 Formica-topped table: (a) orthographic projection, (b) an exploded detail of the construction.

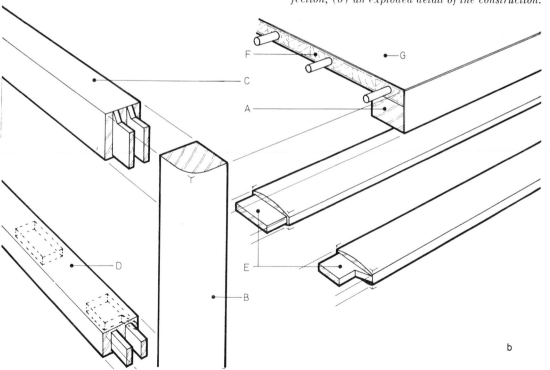

F

C

G

A

D

E

B

b

107

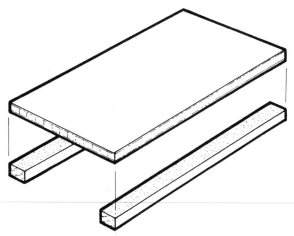

Fig. 109 *Glue the top battens to the blockboard.*

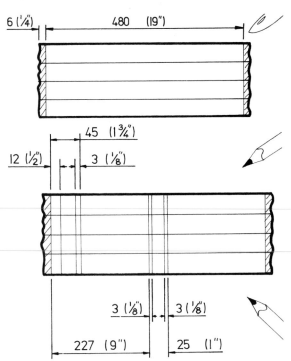

Fig. 111 *Hold the four legs together and mark out the overall length with a knife.*

Use a smoothing plane to plane the edges of the laminate flush with the battens on the underside, and almost flush with the blockboard on the top. The plane blade will need to be frequently sharpened when this is done.

Now mark out and cut the laminate for the top so that it is about $\frac{1}{4}$ in (6 mm) oversize. Glue the laminate in position with contact adhesive, taking care to expel all the air at the center by pressing from the center outwards with your hands.

Carefully trim the edges of the top using a smoothing plane held at a 60° angle (fig. 110).

8) Hold the four legs together face-side downwards, mark the overall length with a knife (fig. 111), and mark out the mortise positions with a pencil. Separate the pieces and square the knife lines around each leg.

9) Place all four end rails together and mark to size with a knife (fig. 112). The rabbet length must be calculated from your work. This distance is approximately $14\frac{1}{8}$ in (359 mm). Square the knife lines around each rail.

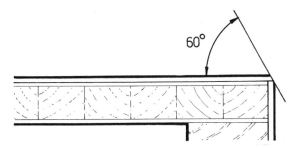

Fig. 110 *Trim the edges of the laminate at 60° with a smoothing plane.*

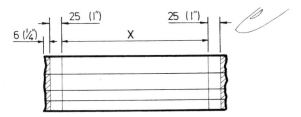

Fig. 112 *Place all four end rails together and mark to size with a knife.*

10) Saw the waste from the ends of the rails.

11) Set the spurs on the mortise gauge to the width apart of your $\frac{1}{4}$-in (6-mm) mortise chisel, then set the stock to within $\frac{5}{16}$ in (8 mm) of the nearest

CONSTRUCTION OF THE FRAME

7) Choose the best surfaces on all the remaining pieces of wood and mark these in pencil with face-side and face-edge marks.

spur. Gauge the twin tenons and their mortises with this setting. Hatch in the waste with a pencil (fig. 113).

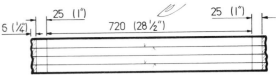

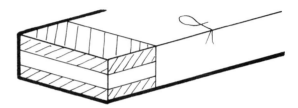

Fig. 115 *Place the slats together and mark them to length with a knife.*

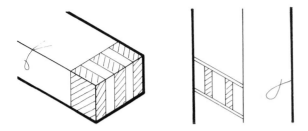

Fig. 113 *Gauge the twin tenons and their mortises.*

12) Chop the mortises 1⅛ in (28 mm) deep (*see* fig. 39). Saw the tenons (*see* figs. 40 & 41). Remove most of the waste between the tenons with a coping saw, then trim back to the line with a mortise chisel. Remove ⅛-in (3-mm) covers from the tenons and cut the sloping haunches. Then fit and number consecutive joints.

13) Place the lower end rails together face-edge downwards and mark out the spacing for the slats in pencil (fig. 114, a). Separate the end rails and gauge the ¼-in (6-mm) mortises centrally along the edge (fig. 114, b).

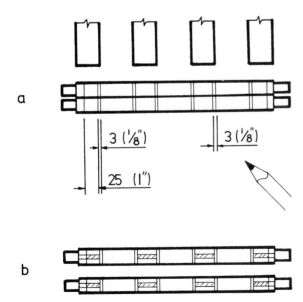

Fig. 114 (a) *Mark out the spacing for the slats on the lower end rails,* (b) *gauge the mortises.*

14) Hold the slats together face-edge upwards and mark out with a knife (fig. 115). Square these knife lines around each slat.

15) Saw the waste from the ends of the slats.

16) Gauge the ¼-in (6-mm) tenons centrally across the ends of the slats. Hatch in the waste with a pencil (fig. 116).

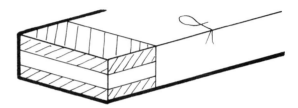

Fig. 116 *Gauge the tenons centrally across the ends of the slats.*

17) Chop the mortises 1⅛ in (28 mm) deep, and saw the tenons. Note that the joint used on the outside slats will be a secret haunched mortise-and-tenon (*see* fig. 44).

18) Clean up all inside—and later inaccessible—surfaces on the end frames by removing a fine shaving all over with the smoothing plane. Round off the sharp corners wherever possible and polish the parts separately.

19) Glue up the end frames one frame at a time. Hold each frame in two bar clamps. Check that each frame is flat by sighting across the legs, and check that the diagonals of each frame measure the same distance. Carefully bend the frames until all is correct, then leave overnight for the glue to set.

20) The shaping of the slats is done in two stages. First, mark out and plane a broad chamfer. Second, round over the corners of the chamfer with a plane, then use some abrasive paper to finish off.

21) Dowel-joint (*see* fig. 33) the frame to the top with five ⅜-in (9-mm) dowels at each end (fig. 108).

22) Clean up the tops of the end frames carefully, and very slightly chamfer the top edge: Chamfer also the laminate top so it joins the end frames making a very small V shape. This helps to disguise any irregularity between the end frames and the laminate top. Clean up all surfaces, and polish them till they're ready for gluing.

Trial-clamp together without glue. If satisfactory, take the pieces apart, swiftly glue the joints, and clamp them together again. Check that the table is square by measuring across the diagonals of the feet.

23) Round over the outside corners of the legs. To do this, draw around a coin or the lid of a can to mark out the curve. Then plane a chamfer, and finish off by rounding the chamfer over with a plane.

TELEVISION TABLE

This television table is very different from other tables, for the top and shelf are cut away to follow the rounded shape of the legs (figs. 117 & 118). In addition, the top is made to finish flush with the tops of the legs. Nearly all television sets arrive with a ready-made table, but here is a table that is at the correct height for comfortable viewing when you are sitting at a dining table or in an armchair. This table also has a shelf that can be used to support a video cassette recorder, or which can just be a convenient spot to put the current edition of the television schedule. The legs of the table are fitted with casters for easy mobility.

The framework of the original television table was made from utile, and the shelves were made from sapele (see Appendix B).

CONSTRUCTION

1) Check the overall dimensions of this table (fig. 117) against the size of your television set before you start construction. If your television set will not fit this table you may have to alter some of the dimensions. Draw a full-size plan (fig. 119).
2) Choose the two best surfaces on each piece of wood and mark these surfaces in pencil with face-side and face-edge marks. Make sure these surfaces are on the outside of the completed table.
3) Hold the legs together, face-sides downward, and mark to length with a knife and mark the joint positions with a pencil (fig. 120).
4) Separate the legs, and square the pencil marks on to one other surface of each leg, but not onto the face-edge.
5) Gauge the ¼-in (6-mm)-wide mortises centrally on the legs using a mortise gauge (fig. 121). The spurs should be set here to the width of your ¼-in (6-mm) mortise chisel.
6) Chop the mortises 1¼ in (30 mm) deep.
7) Mark out and cut a ⅛-in (3-mm)-deep rabbet across the mortises to take the exact width of the rails (fig. 122). The depth of this rabbet was calculated from a full-size cross-sectional drawing of a leg (see fig. 119): You can check the depth of the rabbet against your own drawing.

CUTTING LIST FOR TELEVISION TABLE—planed, finished sizes

Hardwood

key	description	quantity	length	width	thickness
A	legs	4	30 in (760 mm)	2 in (50 mm)	2 in (50 mm)
B	long rails	4	24½ in (620 mm)	2 in (50 mm)	⅞ in (22 mm)
C	short rails	4	18 in (460 mm)	2 in (50 mm)	⅞ in (22 mm)
D	buttons	1	36 in (900 mm)	1¼ in (32 mm)	¾ in (19 mm)
E	top & shelf	2	27½ in (700 mm)	20 in (510 mm)	¾ in (19 mm)

Hardware

16 brass flathead screws 1¼ in (32 mm) × no. 8
4 peg-fitting casters 2 in (50 mm) high

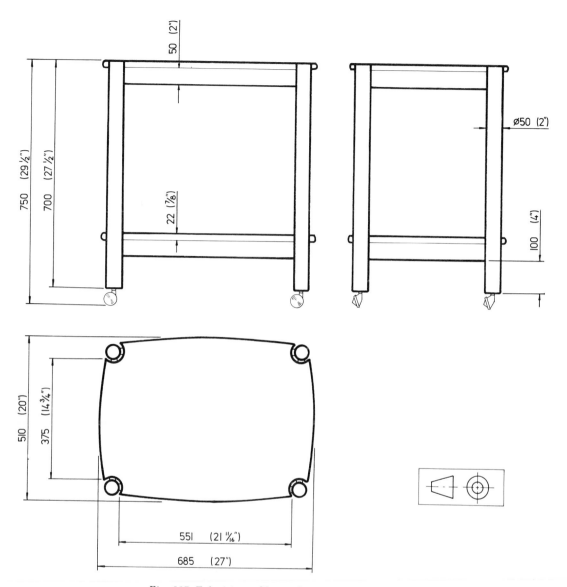

Fig. 117 Television table: orthographic projection.

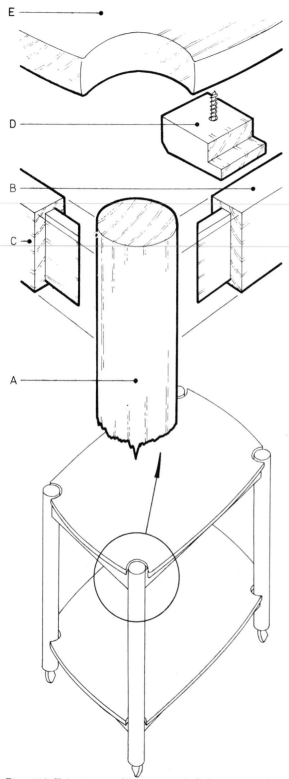

E

D

B

C

A

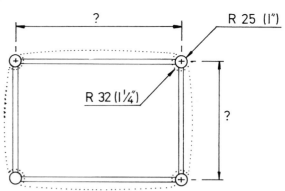

R 25 (1″)

R 32 (1¼″)

?

?

Fig. 119 Draw a full-size sketch of the table plan.

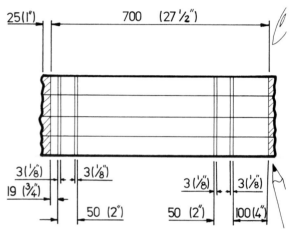

25 (1″)

700   (27½″)

3 (⅛″)   3 (⅛″)

19 (¾″)

50 (2″)

3 (⅛″)   3 (⅛″)

50 (2″)   100 (4″)

Fig. 120 Hold the legs together: Mark to length with a knife and mark the joint positions with a pencil.

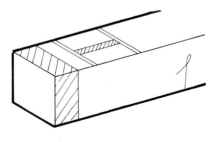

Fig. 121 Gauge the mortises centrally on the legs with a mortise gauge.

Fig. 118 Television table: an exploded view of the construction.

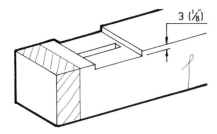

Fig. 122 Mark out and cut a rabbet across the mortises to take the exact width of the rails.

8) Round off the legs by: a) marking out a hexagon at each end of the legs and removing the corners with a plane, and b) removing the corners of the hexagon with a plane until the rabbet measures $\frac{7}{8}$ in (22 mm) wide (fig. 123). Woodworkers who own a woodturning lathe can use it to round off the legs. The original table, however, was made without using a lathe.

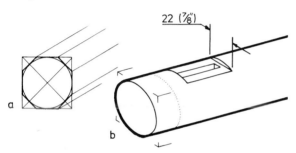

Fig. 123 Rounding off the legs: (a) mark out a hexagon on the ends of the legs, and plane the legs to the hexagonal shape, (b) remove the corners from the hexagon until the legs are round.

9) Mark the rails to length (fig. 124).
10) Separate the rails and square the knife lines around each rail. Saw the waste from the ends of the rails.

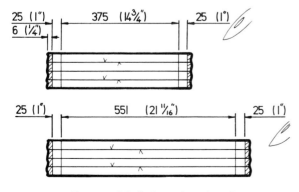

Fig. 124 Mark the rails to length.

11) Gauge the $\frac{1}{4}$-in-(6-mm) thick tenons centrally on the ends of the rails with a mortise gauge (fig. 125).

Fig. 125 Gauge the tenons centrally on the ends of the rails.

12) Cut the tenons in the normal way (see figs. 40 & 41) and remove $\frac{1}{8}$-in (3-mm) covers.
13) Miter the ends of the tenons so they do not quite touch each other inside the mortises (fig. 126).

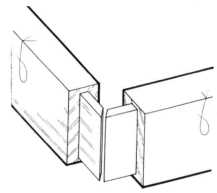

Fig. 126 Miter the ends of the tenons so that they do not touch inside the mortises.

14) Assemble the table without glue, and check that all the joints fit. Number adjacent joints.
15) Mark out and cut three button slots (fig. 127)

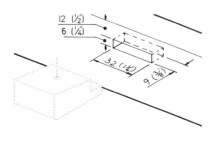

Fig. 127 A button slot.

along the inside of the long rails. Similarly mark out and cut one button slot on the inside of each short rail.

16) Clean up all surfaces till they're ready for gluing.

17) Glue up the large frames with clamps to pull the work together. Check that each frame is square by measuring the diagonals, and check that each frame is flat by sighting across the rails. Carefully bend the frames until they are correct. Wipe away the surplus glue with a damp rag, and let the glue set overnight.

18) Glue the short rails into their mortises, and clamp the framework together. Check that the framework is square by measuring across the diagonals, and check that it is not twisted by sighting across the rails. Carefully bend the framework until all is correct. Wipe off surplus glue with a damp rag, and leave the framework for the glue to dry.

19) Polish the framework. The original table was polished using three coats of Danish oil with drying time between each coat; then the wood was given a coat of wax polish.

20) Make the sixteen buttons, and polish them till they're ready for attaching to the top of the table (fig. 128).

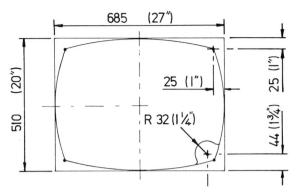

Fig. 129 *Mark out the shape of the top and the shelf.*

from the corners of the wood to find points that can be used as centers of curves with radiuses of 1¼ in (32 mm) (fig. 129).

22) Shape the top and the shelf with either a coping saw or a bandsaw. Clean up the edges with a spokeshave. The shaped corners on the original table were cleaned up with a home-made drum sander fitted into the chuck on an electric drill. The drum sander consisted of a bolt, two large washers, a cylindrical piece of reconstituted upholstery foam, and a strip of abrasive paper which was glued around on itself to form a drum (fig. 130). This produced excellent results.

A slight barrelling of the edges on the top and shelf will help to improve your result.

23) Clean up and polish the top and shelf, then attach them both to the framework with the sixteen buttons and wood screws.

24) Attach casters to the feet of the table.

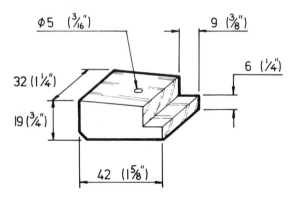

Fig. 128 *A button used to fix the top and the shelf to the framework.*

21) Prepare the top and shelf, 27 in (690 mm) long by 20 in (510 mm) wide. Measure 1 in (25 mm) in from all four corners: Using a thin lath of wood as a guide, join these points to the centers of the sides in a smooth curve. Now measure 1¾ in (45 mm) in

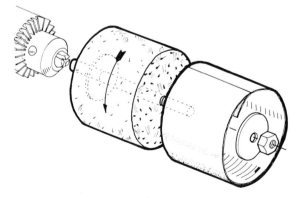

Fig. 130 *A home-made drum sanding machine.*

CORNER CABINET

This corner cabinet (figs. 131 & 132) is a secure and attractive way to display articles of silver, glass and porcelain. Inside the cabinet there are two glass shelves that can be adjusted in height, and the back of the cabinet has two panels which are covered with baize: These baize-covered panels make an excellent background for any display. On completion, either the corner cabinet can be screwed into the corner of a wall, or you may decide to continue the work by designing and building a base unit on which the cabinet can stand.

The design idea for the original corner cabinet was given to me by Frank James. The original cabinet was made from mahogany, and the panels on the inside were lined with green baize. The hinge and the lock were of solid brass.

CUTTING LIST FOR CORNER CABINET—planed, finished sizes

Hardwood

key	description	quantity	length	width	thickness
A	sides	2	33 in (820 mm)	2¾ in (70 mm)	¾ in (20 mm)
B	front frame uprights	2	33 in (820 mm)	1⅝ in (40 mm)	¾ in (20 mm)
C	front frame rails	2	18 in (450 mm)	2⅜ in (60 mm)	¾ in (20 mm)
D	back uprights	2	33 in (820 mm)	1⅝ in (40 mm)	¾ in (20 mm)
E	back uprights	2	33 in (820 mm)	2 in (50 mm)	¾ in (20 mm)
F	back rails	4	15 in (360 mm)	2⅜ in (60 mm)	¾ in (20 mm)
G	door stiles	2	28 in (700 mm)	1 in (25 mm)	¾ in (20 mm)
H	door rails	2	16 in (400 mm)	1⅝ in (40 mm)	¾ in (20 mm)
I	moulding	1	28 in (700 mm)	¾ in (20 mm)	¾ in (20 mm)

Blockboard—hardwood veneered

key	description	quantity	length	width	thickness
J	top & bottom	1	32 in (800 mm)	12 in (300 mm)	¾ in (20 mm)

Plywood or fibreboard (hardboard)

key	description	quantity	length	width	thickness
K	panels	4	28 in (700 mm)	12¼ in (310 mm)	⅛ in (3 mm)

Hardware

1 brass piano hinge 28 in (700 mm) long, with ⅝-in (16-mm) brass screws to fit
5 brass flathead screws 1 in (25 mm) × no. 6
2 pieces of ⅙-in (4-mm) glass cut to template shape for shelves with ground and polished edges
6 shelf studs
1 piece of 1/10-in (2-mm) glass cut to fit the door
14 ½-in (12-mm) brads (panel pins)
1 small brass-door lock

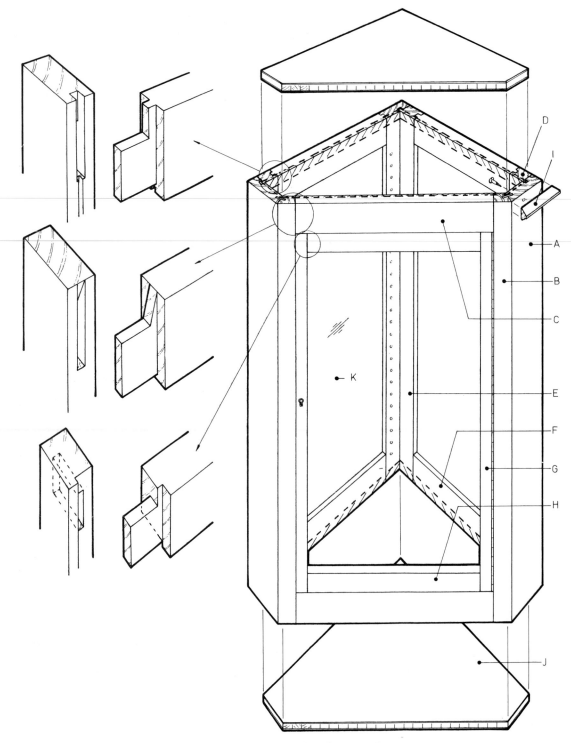

Fig. 131 Corner cabinet: An exploded view of the construction.

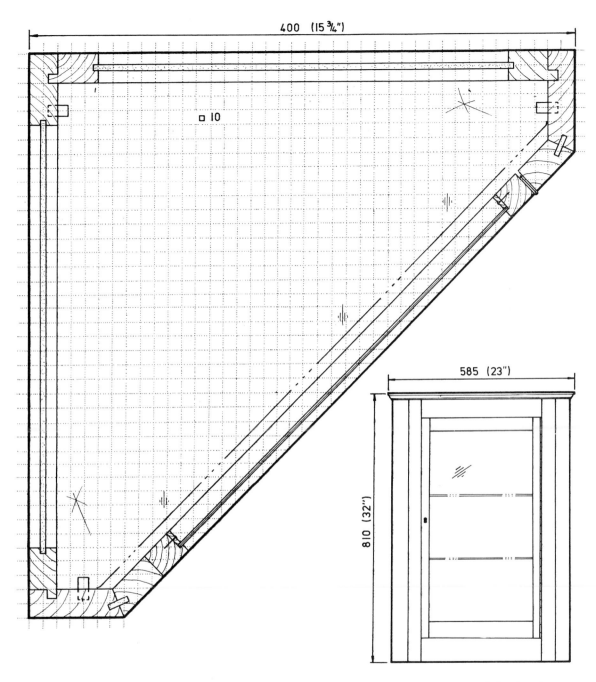

400 (15¾")

□ 10

585 (23")

810 (32")

Fig. 132 *Corner cabinet: The plan view drawn over a grid of .4-in (10-mm) squares, and the elevation.*

1) Draw a full-size cross-sectional view of the cabinet (fig. 132) so that the sizes and angles can be accurately obtained.

2) Sort out the wood you have bought so that you can identify each piece; arrange things so that the best pieces of wood will be at the front of the cabinet. Mark each piece of wood in pencil with a face-side and a face-edge mark.

3) The construction starts with the front frame: This is not the door, but the frame that surrounds the door.

4) The front frame should be constructed with secret haunched mortise-and-tenon joints (see fig. 44). The external dimensions of the frame should be 32 in (810 mm) × 18½ in (470 mm).

a) Hold the front-frame rails together, and mark out with a knife (fig. 133). Then separate the rails and square the knife lines around both of the rails. Cut the waste from the ends.

b) Hold the front-frame uprights together, and mark out (fig. 134). Square the knife lines around both of the uprights, but leave the pencil lines confined to the face edges.

c) Set the mortise gauge so that the spurs are ¼ in (6 mm) apart; then gauge the mortises centrally on the frame uprights, and gauge the tenons on the ends of the front frame rails.

d) Chop the mortises 1⅛ in (28 mm) deep, and remove the waste to make the secret haunch. Saw the tenons, then mark out and cut the secret haunches on the tenons. Fit the joints together.

e) Clean up the inside surfaces on the front frame: Then polish these surfaces and glue up. Check that the frame is square by measuring the diagonals, and check that the frame is flat by sighting across from one rail to another. Carefully bend the frame until it is correct, then leave it alone for the glue to dry.

5) Obtain the angle between the front frame and the sides from your full-size cross-sectional drawing: This angle should be about 67½°.

The frame and the sides should be planed to this angle. This is not easy to do by hand, but it is made very easy with a machine planer. People without a planing machine could try using a radial arm saw or a bandsaw. When using a machine cut just outside of the line, and finish to the line using a hand plane.

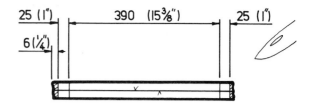

Fig. 133 Hold the front-frame rails together and mark out with a knife.

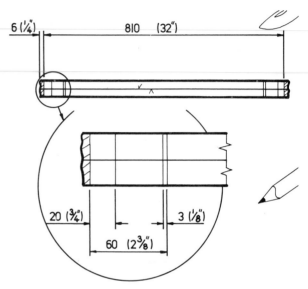

Fig. 134 Hold the front-frame uprights together and mark them out.

The joint obtained can be further strengthened with a ⅛-in (3-mm)-thick plywood tongue. This involves making a groove ⅛ in (3 mm) wide × ¼ in (6 mm) deep in the edge of the front frame and in the edge of the sides. Again, this is not particularly easy to do, and it does require skill and patience.

6) Make a ¼-in (6-mm) × ¼-in (6-mm) groove on sides—the groove should be 9/16 in (14 mm) from the edge of the wood. This groove will later accommodate the back frames.

7) Trim the waste from the ends of the front frame. Mark out and cut the sides to the same length as the front frame.

8) Work is now going to continue with the back frames.

a) Note that each back frame has a 1⅝-in (40-mm)-

and a 2-in (50-mm)-wide upright; this is so that a tongue-and-groove can be worked in the back corner to hold the frames together.

b) Hold the four uprights together and mark them out (fig. 135). Square the knife lines all around each piece, but leave the pencil lines confined to the face edges.

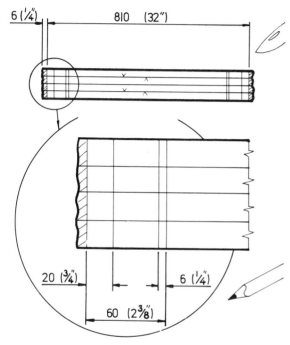

Fig. 135 Hold the four uprights together and mark them out.

c) Hold the back rails together and mark with a knife (fig. 136). Separate the pieces and square the knife lines around each rail. Saw the waste from the ends of the rails.

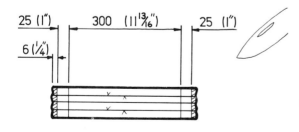

Fig. 136 Hold the back rails together and mark them with a knife.

d) Set the mortise gauge so that the spurs are $\frac{1}{4}$ in (6 mm) apart; gauge for the mortises on the back uprights, and for the tenons on the ends of the rails.

e) Chop the mortises $1\frac{1}{8}$ in (28 mm) deep and remove the waste for the square haunch. Saw the tenons, then mark out and cut the square haunches on the tenons. Fit all the joints.

f) Make a groove $\frac{1}{8}$ in (3 mm) square on the inside edges of the frame to receive the plywood or fibreboard (hardboard) panels that make up the back.

g) Fit the panels with the smooth surface on the outside of the cabinet.

h) Take the frames apart. Clean up and polish the inside edges of the frames.

i) Glue up the frames with the panels in position. Hold each frame in bar clamps to make sure that each joint is fully closed. Check that each frame is square by measuring the diagonals, and check that each frame is flat by sighting across the uprights. Carefully twist each frame until each is correct, then leave for the glue to dry.

j) Clean up the frames by removing one or two thin shavings all over with a smoothing plane.

k) Rabbet and groove the edges of the back frames so that they fit together as per your cross-sectional drawing.

9) Trim the waste from the ends of all the pieces used so far. Then mark out and cut a rabbet $\frac{3}{4}$ in (18 mm) × $\frac{1}{8}$ in (4 mm) so that the top and bottom pieces can later be dropped/pushed into place. These parts will later be held in those rabbets merely by glue.

10) Mark out accurately and drill for the shelf studs. If a series of holes are drilled at 1-in (25-mm) centers the shelves will be adjustable.

11) Polish all the inside surfaces till they're ready for gluing up.

12) Clamp the cabinet together without glue; this is to find out any snags, as it is quite a complex structure to put together. Use your ingenuity with the clamps. Some people like to glue blocks of wood onto the job in order to get a straight pull with the clamps, and then to remove these blocks at a later stage.

My method is to glue and clamp the back corner joint, then let the glue set for several hours. Then I glue one of the sides, and clamp it to the back structure. Again, time is allowed for the glue to dry.

Finally, the remaining side and the front frame are quickly glued together; bar clamps and two lengths of rope placed around the outside of the cabinet and tightened tourniquet fashion are used to hold the work together. Make sure that the rabbets at the top and bottom remain level.

13) Clean up the outside of the cabinet so it's ready for polishing.

14) Make a moulding from the length of ¾-in (20-mm) × ¾-in (20-mm)-section hardwood. This is done in two stages (fig. 137). First, cut two rabbets ½ in (12 mm) × ⅛ in (3 mm). Second, shape the curve with either the rabbet plane or a moulding plane.

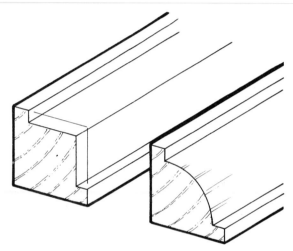

Fig. 137 Making the moulding from hardwood.

Fit the moulding to the cabinet: Glue it, position around the top of the cabinet, and screw it from the inside.

15) Polish the outside of the cabinet.

16) Cut and fit the top and bottom pieces so that they are push-fitted into the rabbets. Polish both sides of these pieces, then glue them permanently in place.

17) Work is now going to continue with the door.

a) Cut the piano hinge to length and fix it temporarily in position with three screws. Fitting the hinge accurately is important if the door is to work well, so take care to line up the center of the pin that runs through the hinge with the corner of the cabinet. Mark the centers of the three screw holes with a pointed instrument, and drill the correct size

of hole for the screws; you may have to drill a short clearance hole for the shank of the screw, as well as a longer and finer pilot hole for the thread part of the screw.

b) Measure the cabinet to discover the exact size for the door. The door will be made just a trifle oversize to allow for cleaning up the edges and fitting it to the cabinet. These are the features you should measure: 1) the height of the cabinet, H; mark the stiles a trifle longer than this (fig. 138). Complete the marking-out of the stiles (fig. 139).

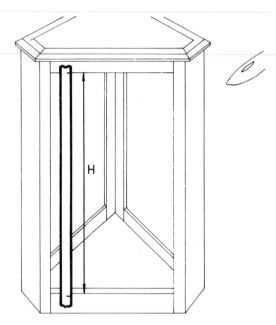

Fig. 138 Mark the stiles a little longer.

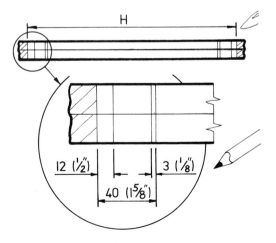

Fig. 139 Complete the marking-out of the stiles.

2) the cross width of the opening, W, with the stiles in position; mark the rails a trifle longer than this (fig. 140). Complete the marking-out of the rails (fig. 141). Cut the waste from the ends of the rails.
c) Set the spurs on the mortise gauge to the width of the ¼-in (6·mm) mortise chisel, and set the stock of the gauge so that the spurs mark centrally along the edge of the wood.

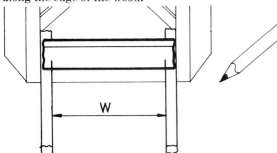

Fig. 140 Mark the door rails a little longer.

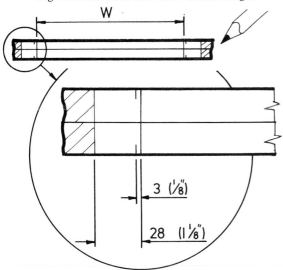

3 (⅛")

28 (1⅛")

Fig. 141 Complete the marking-out of the door rails.

d) Gauge the mortises on both edges of the stiles, then gauge the tenons. Complete the marking-out with a knife (fig. 142).
e) Chop the mortises ⅝ in (15 mm) deep from each edge of the wood so that each mortise is a through mortise (i.e., it passes right through the wood). Cut the tenons (fig. 143).
f) Rabbet the stiles and rails ½ in (13 mm) × ⅛ in (3 mm), and trim the tenons to fit the mortises (fig. 144).
g) Clean up and polish the inside surfaces of the door, then glue it up and clamp the parts together.

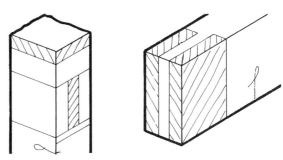

Fig. 142 Gauge the mortises and the tenons.

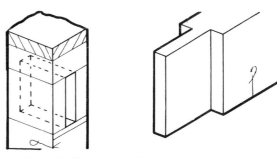

Fig. 143 Chop the mortises and saw the tenons.

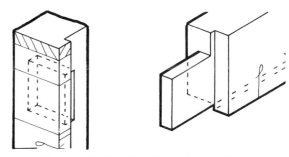

Fig. 144 Rabbet the stiles and the rails.

Check that the door is square by measuring the diagonals, and check that it is flat by sighting across the rails. Leave the door in clamps for the glue to set.
h) Clean up the door frame with a finely set smoothing plane.
18) The door must now be fitted to the cabinet. Make sure the same amount of waste is removed from both of the stiles and both of the rails. Otherwise, things will look unbalanced. Fitting starts (*see* fig. 145) by planing: a) the hinge stile, b) the bottom edge of the door to fit the cabinet, c) the top edge of the door to fit the cabinet, and d) the lock stile to fit the cabinet. Finally, the lock stile is trimmed slightly out of square (fig. 146) so that the door closes properly.
19) Remove the hinge from the cabinet and fit it to the door with three screws—so that the center of

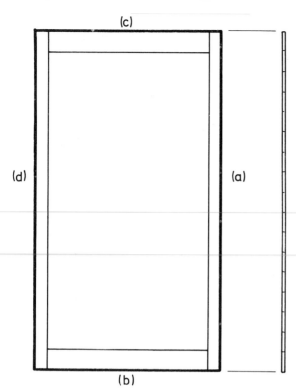

(c)

(d)   (a)

(b)

Fig. 145 *Trim the edges of the door in the sequence:*
(a), (b), (c), (d).

Fig. 146 *The lock stile is trimmed slightly out-of-*
square.

the hinge pin is in line with the corner of the door.
Fix the hinge onto the cabinet and try closing the
door to test for fit. Make any adjustments that are
needed. The screw positions can be moved by using
a bradawl or other sharp-pointed instrument to push
the wood fibres from one side of the screw hole to
the other: This is called pelleting the screw hole.
Polish the door, hang it permanently, and fit the
lock.

20) Two door stops are needed to prevent the door
from being pushed too far into the cabinet. These
can be made from offcuts of the brass hinge (fig.
147).

Fix one door stop at the top of the cabinet and
one at the bottom of the cabinet, so that they both
contact with the locking stile when the door is
closed. You will not be able to get a screwdriver
inside the cabinet, so use $\frac{5}{8}$-in (15-mm) brass nails;
squeeze them into the work with a C clamp. Place a
large piece of scrap wood on the front of the cabinet
to prevent the shoe of the C clamp from marking the
cabinet. This may seem an unusual method, but it
works perfectly well. Bending the top of the brass
strip allows for any fine adjustments that are needed.

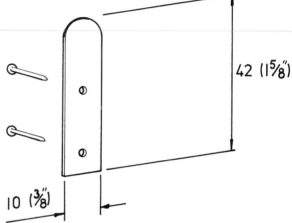

42 $(1\frac{5}{8}")$

10 $(\frac{3}{8}")$

Fig. 147 *Make two door stops from offcuts of the*
brass hinge.

21) Locks look better when the keyhole is fitted with
an escutcheon—this is a small piece of brass bought
ready-made in a keyhole shape. Tap the escutcheon
against the wood with a hammer; this leaves an im-
pression of the hole that needs to be drilled and the
shape of the slot that needs to be cut with a coping
saw. Drill the hole first, then thread the blade of the
coping saw through the hole and cut out the keyhole
shape. Glue the escutcheon in position with epoxy
resin adhesive.

22) Place the glass in the rabbet for the door. Fix
the glass in place with glazing strip. The glazing
strip needs mitering at the corners, and $\frac{1}{2}$-in (12-
mm) brads are used to fix the strip using the edge
of a large firmer chisel; slide the chisel against the
glass so that it acts the same way as a hammer, and
the same way it would if you were picture-framing.

23) If the door is a very good fit you may need
a $\frac{3}{8}$-in (9-mm) diameter hole through the base of

the cabinet as an air escape to make opening and shutting the door easier.

24) Trim the two spare fibreboard (hardboard) panels so they are a loose fit on the frames inside the cabinet. The fibreboard panels can be covered with material—green baize Fablon™ was used on the original, and a margin of 1 in (25 mm) was wrapped onto the back of the fibreboard (hardboard).* Glue the panels into the cabinet with contact adhesive.

25) Cut a fibreboard (hardboard) template for the shelves; try this in place before ordering the glass. One-eighth-in (4-mm) glass is required here with a ground and polished edge.

26) The cabinet can be fixed to the wall with flush cabinet mounts.

FIRESIDE CHAIR

This fireside chair (figs. 148 & 149) is of open framework construction and has a Scandinavian appearance. The seat cushion is supported by six strands of rubber webbing, but the back cushion rests against a framework fitted with four wooden slats. Many of the wooden surfaces are shaped or rounded to make them more comfortable, and to give a neat appearance.

The two cushions are identical, and can be fitted with covers that can be unzipped for easy washing or dry cleaning.

The original chair was made from mahogany, and had pale lemon-yellow cushion covers.

CUTTING LIST FOR FIRESIDE CHAIR—planed, finished sizes

Hardwood

key	description	quantity	length	width	thickness
A	legs	4	21 in (540 mm)	1½ in (38 mm)	1¹/₁₆ in (27 mm)
B	side rails	2	25 in (640 mm)	3 in (76 mm)	⅞ in (22 mm)
C	arms	2	27½ in (700 mm)	3 in (76 mm)	1 in (25 mm)
D	front rail	1	22 in (560 mm)	3 in (76 mm)	⅞ in (22 mm)
E	back frame	1	20½ in (520 mm)	2⅞ in (73 mm)	⅞ in (22 mm)
	back frame	4	20½ in (520 mm)	2⅛ in (54 mm)	⅞ in (22 mm)
F	back splats	4	18 in (460 mm)	1⅛ in (29 mm)	⅝ in (16 mm)
G	webbing rails	2	19 in (480 mm)	1 in (25 mm)	⅝ in (16 mm)

Hardware

10 ft (3 m) of 2-in (25-mm) wide rubber webbing
12 steel webbing clips
12 steel roundhead screws ¾ in (19 mm) × no. 6
2 pieces of medium-density upholstery foam 20 in (510 mm) × 20 in (510 mm) × 3 in (76 mm)
2 tailored zip-on covers

* Fablon is an adhesive plastic covering which is available in many colors and patterns.

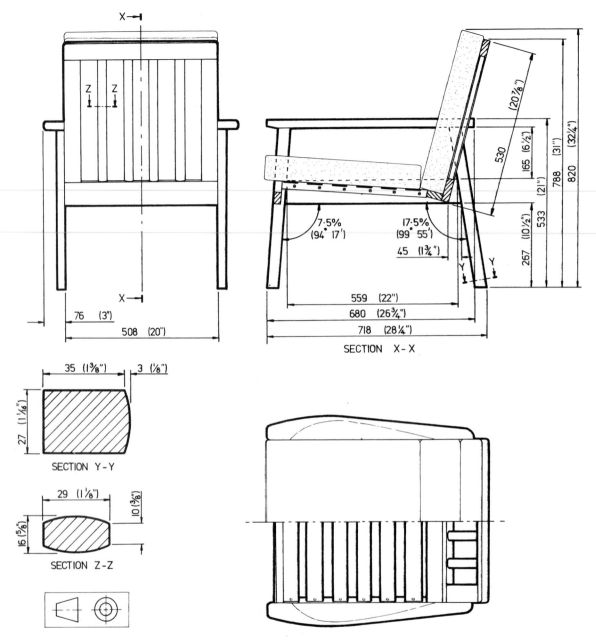

Fig. 148 Fireside chair: orthographic projection.

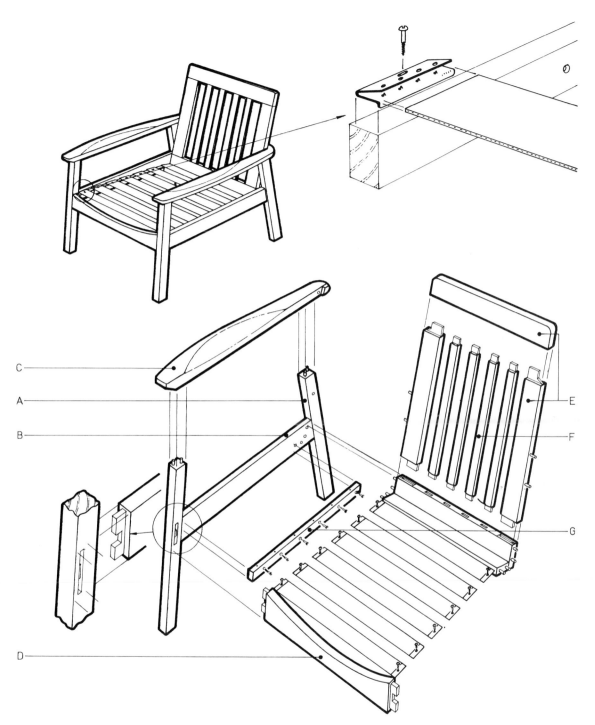

Fig. 149 Fireside chair: A pictorial view with a detail showing how the webbing is attached to the frame, and an exploded view of the construction.

CONSTRUCTION OF THE SIDE FRAMES

1) Choose the best surfaces for the outside, and mark these in pencil with face-side and face-edge marks. Place the side rails together in the vise, and mark them to length (fig. 150). A special tool called a sliding T bevel can help you mark lines at an angle of other than 90°.

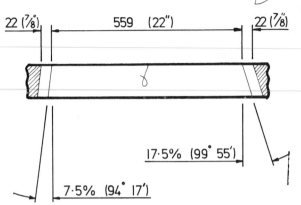

Fig. 150 *Place the side rails together in the vise and mark them to length.*

2) Saw the waste from the ends of the side rails.
3) Hold the four legs together face-side downwards. Place one side rail across the legs, and transfer the width of the rail onto the legs with a pencil (fig. 151). Mark a further line ⅛ in (3 mm) inside of each line to allow a cover over the joint as a means of concealment. Then divide the mortise into three equal parts—this is to conserve the strength of the leg.

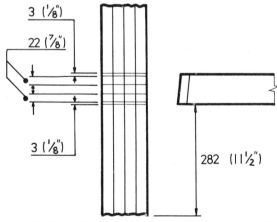

Fig. 151 *Hold the legs together and transfer the width of the side rail onto the legs with a pencil.*

Set the distance between the spurs of the mortise gauge to the width of the ¼-in (6-mm) mortise chisel. Then adjust the stock until the gauge marks centrally down the edge of the side rail. Gauge the rails, and then the legs, with this setting—take care with the legs, for they are now irreversible.

4) Cut the tenons in the usual way (*see* figs. 40 & 41).

5) Transfer the covers and the haunch from the legs onto the tenons (fig. 152). Cut out the waste, using a backsaw and coping saw.

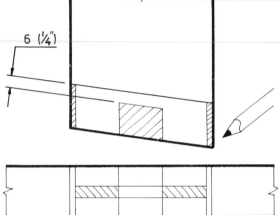

Fig. 152 *Transfer the covers and the haunch from the legs onto the tenons.*

6) Chop the mortises to a depth of 1 in (25 mm) (*see* fig. 39), but take care to slope the ends of each mortise correctly.

7) Clean up and polish the inside surfaces, then glue up—you may find wedge-shaped clamping blocks useful here.

8) When the glue has set, mark the legs to length with a long batten and a knife (fig. 153). Saw off the waste from both ends of each leg.

9) Tap two brads into the top of each leg, and snip the heads off just above the wood (fig. 154). Press each arm down in its correct position. The brads will mark the correct position for the dowels. Remove the brads and bore ⅜-in (9-mm) diameter holes for the dowels. Cut the dowel to length—a saw cut in the side of the dowel will allow excess glue to escape from the joint.

10) Mark out a shape on the arms with a pencil (fig. 155). Cut the shape with a coping saw and spokeshave. Hollowing the arm may prove difficult,

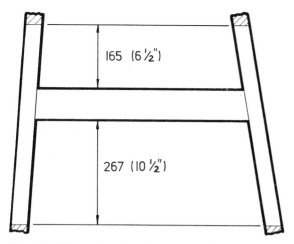

Fig. 153 When the glue has set, mark the legs to length with a long batten and a knife.

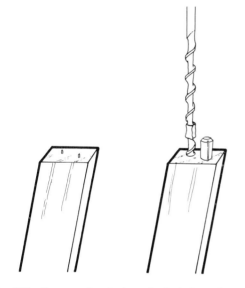

Fig. 154 Tap two brads (panel pins) into the top of each leg and snip the heads off the pins just above the wood.

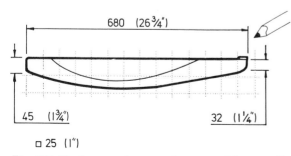

Fig. 155 Mark out a shape on the arms with a pencil.

but an effective method is to use the flat metal spokeshave with the blade reversed (i.e., with the blade bevel upwards). The spokeshave will then scrape the wood and leave a clean finish regardless of the grain direction.

11) Clean up and polish the arms and the side frames, then glue up.

CONSTRUCTION OF THE FRONT RAIL AND BACK FRAME

12) Mark out the front rail (fig. 156), then saw the waste from the ends.

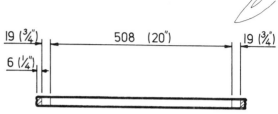

Fig. 156 Mark out the front rail.

13) Use a pencil to mark out the mortise limit lines on the side frames. Gauge the mortises and the tenons.

14) Cut the tenons, and then chop the mortises $\frac{7}{8}$ in (22 mm) deep.

15) Use a bent lath of wood to mark out the curve on the top edge of the front rail. The curve should be $1\frac{1}{4}$ in (32 mm) at the center point. Shape the curve with a coping saw and spokeshave.

16) The back is constructed as one frame (fig. 149). The frame has to be 21 in (533 mm) high × 20 in (508 mm) wide overall.

17) The lower rail of the back frame has another rail dowelled and glued to it; this secondary rail will support the lower edge of the back cushion and will give rigidity to the frame.

18) Polish the parts of the back individually, then glue them together. Clean up the outside of the frame and complete the polishing.

19) Place the back at the correct angle to the side frames (fig. 148), and use brads to locate the dowel positions (fig. 149). The brads can be removed and holes bored for the dowels.

WEBBING

20) Scrape back an area of polish on the side

frames, and glue and screw on the webbing rails so that they fall by about 2 in (50 mm) at the back.

21) Cut six pieces of rubber webbing 18 in (457 mm) long. Clamp the metal clips onto the ends of the webbing, taking care that the rounded edge on each clip can be positioned downwards on the seat.

22) Fix each clip to the webbing rail with a ¾-in (19-mm) no. 6 gauge steel roundhead screw. The webbing must be stretched across the seat; the correct allowance has already been made for this.

CUSHIONS

23) Each cushion measures 20 in (510 mm) × 20 in (510 mm) × 3 in (76 mm), and can be made by covering medium-density polyurethane foam with a tailored zip-on cover.

CUTTING LIST FOR CARVER CHAIR (OPPOSITE PAGE)—planed, finished sizes

Hardwood

key	description	quantity	length	width	thickness
A	back legs	2	30 in (760 mm)	1¾ in (45 mm)	1⅛ in (29 mm)
B	front legs	2	25 in (640 mm)	1¾ in (45 mm)	1⅛ in (29 mm)
C	side rails	2	18 in (460 mm)	2½ in (64 mm)	⅞ in (22 mm)
D	arms	2	19 in (480 mm)	1¾ in (45 mm)	⅞ in (22 mm)
E	front and back rails	2	21 in (530 mm)	3 in (76 mm)	⅞ in (22 mm)
F	back rest	2	21 in (530 mm)	1¾ in (45 mm)	1¾ in (45 mm)
G	seat rails	2	18 in (460 mm)	1¼ in (32 mm)	¾ in (19 mm)

Dowel

		quantity	length	width	
		1	12 in (300 mm)	¼-in (6-mm) diameter	

Plywood

H	seat	5	20 in (510 mm)	4 in (100 mm)	⅜ in (9 mm)

Dense-chip upholstery foam (i.e., reconstituted foam)

	quantity	length	width	thickness
	1	20 in (510 mm)	20 in (510 mm)	1 in (25 mm)

Medium-density upholstery foam

	quantity	length	width	thickness
	1	25 in (640 mm)	20 in (510 mm)	1 in (25 mm)

Plastic upholstery, or upholstery hide

	quantity	length	width
	1	28 in (710 mm)	28 in (710 mm)

Hardware

10 brass flathead screws 1 in (25 mm) × no. 8
 4 brass flathead screws 1¼ in (32 mm) × no. 8
 8 metal blazer-type buttons ¾-in (19-mm) diameter

CARVER CHAIR
(see cutting list, page 128)

This comfortable, low-back carver chair (figs. 157 & 158) has curved back-rails and a dished seat. Five strips of plywood supported by two hollowed-out wooden rails make the task of constructing the seat very easy.

The original carver chair was made from teak, and the seat was upholstered in dark green hide—though a plastic upholstery material could also be used. Four buttons covered with leather help to give the seat a neat appearance.

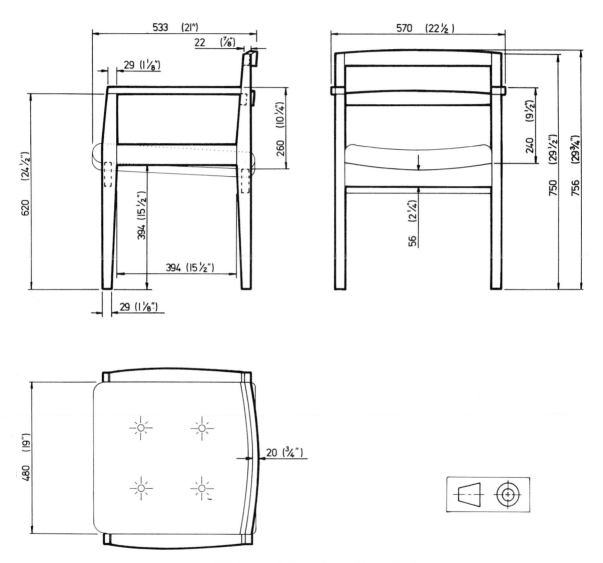

Fig. 157 Carver chair: orthographic projection.

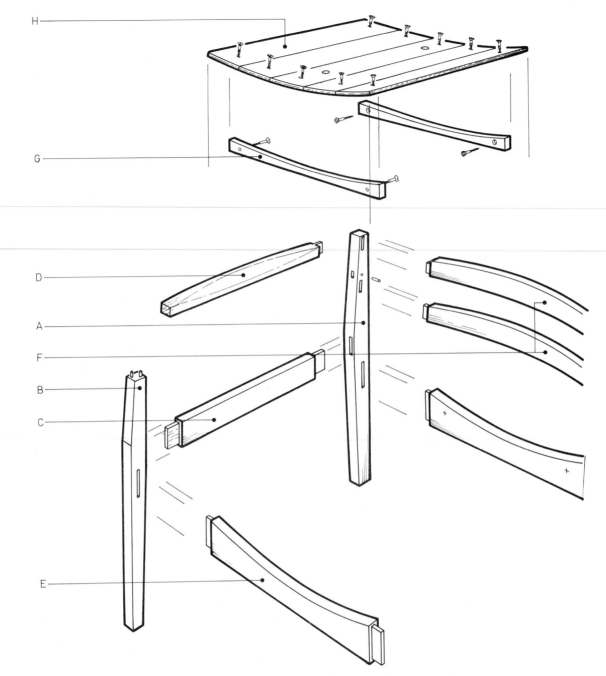

Fig. 158 Carver chair: An exploded view of the construction.

CONSTRUCTION OF THE SIDE FRAMES

1) Sort out the wood for the legs, side rails, and arms. Choose the best surfaces on each piece of wood; you can make sure these surfaces will be on the outside of the chair by marking them in pencil with face-side and face-edge marks.

2) Hold the legs together face-edges downwards, and mark out the mortise positions in pencil (fig. 159); mark the pieces to length with a knife. Hatch in the waste. Square the knife lines around each leg.

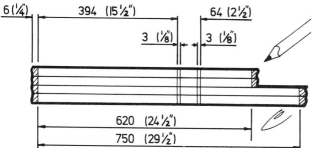

Fig. 159 Hold the legs together, face-edges downward and mark out the mortise positions in pencil; mark the legs to length with a knife.

3) Hold the side rails together, and mark out the lengths of the tenons with a knife (fig. 160). Separate the rails and square the knife lines around each piece. Cut the ¼-in (6 mm) waste from the ends of the side rails.

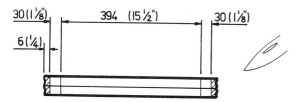

Fig. 160 Hold the side rails together and mark out the lengths of the tenons with a knife.

4) Set the spurs on the mortise gauge the same distance apart as the ¼-in (6-mm) mortise chisel, then set the gauge to work centrally along the edges of the rails. Use this setting to gauge the tenons on the side rails (fig. 161), and gauge the mortises on the legs from the insides of the legs. Hatch in the waste areas with a pencil, then check before you start cutting the joints that the frames will finish flat on the inside.

5) Chop the mortises 1¼ in (32 mm) deep, and cut the tenons. Remove the ⅛-in (3-mm) cover from both edges of the tenons, and fit the joints together without glue. Number the joints A-A, B-B, and so on.

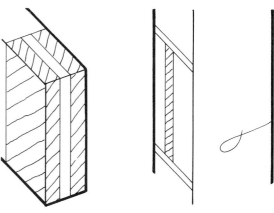

Fig. 161 Gauge the tenons on the side rails and gauge the mortises on the legs.

6) With the side frames loosely assembled, mark out the shaping on the legs (fig. 162). Saw to within ⅛ in (3 mm) of your lines, then carefully plane away the remaining waste.

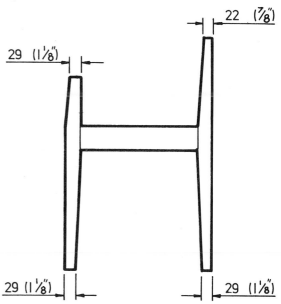

Fig. 162 With the side frames loosely assembled, mark out the shaping on the legs.

7) Accurately remove the waste from the top of the front leg. Assemble each frame and strike a line across the back leg. This line must be level with the top of the front leg, and it must be parallel to the side rail. Draw another line ⅞ in (22 mm) above that line—this being the thickness of the arm. Gauge a ¼-in (6-mm) mortise in the center of the leg. Chop the mortise ⅞ in (22 mm) deep (fig. 163).

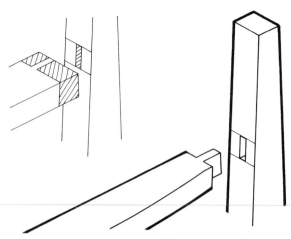

Fig. 163 *Mark out and cut the mortise and tenons that join the arm to the leg.*

8) A sliding T bevel—a kind of try square that can be adjusted to all angles—is useful when marking out the rabbet line of the tenon on the arm. Take the angle of slope off the back leg. Use a try square to help square the marks across the top and the underside of the arm.

9) When the joints between the arm and back leg fit correctly, tap two brads into the top of each leg in positions that are suitable for ¼-in (6-mm) dowels. Nip the heads from the brads, leaving about ⅛ in (3 mm) of each brad standing above the wood. Press each arm down onto the brads. This will accurately mark out the dowel positions. Withdraw the brads, then drill and fit short lengths of dowel in their place (fig. 164).

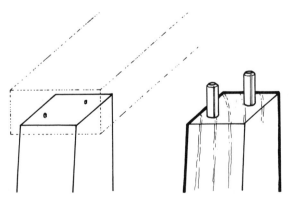

Fig. 164 *Fit small pieces of dowel in place of the brads.*

10) Shape the arm on the outside edge by bending a thin lath of wood and drawing around the lath with a pencil. The top of the arm can either be kept flat or very slightly hollowed. A spokeshave in which the blade has been turned upside down will be found useful when hollowing the wood.

11) Prepare the side frames for gluing: Clean up the surfaces that will be awkward to get at after gluing up, round off all sharp corners where possible, and polish the parts where they have been cleaned up. The original carver chair was made in teak, but because this is a difficult wood to glue, the chair was not polished until after gluing up in order that the polish would not shorten the chances of the glue holding well.

Glue up one frame at a time. Check carefully that each frame is true in every way before you leave the work for the glue to dry.

CONSTRUCTION OF THE CROSS RAILS

12) Hold the four cross rails (i.e., the front and back rails, and the backrest) together and mark out the lengths of the tenons with a knife (fig. 165).

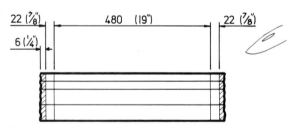

Fig. 165 *Holding the four cross rails together, mark out the lengths of the tenons with a knife.*

Separate the pieces and square the knife lines around each piece. Cut the waste from the ends.

13) Set the spurs on the mortise gauge to the same disance apart as your ¼-in (6-mm) mortise chisel, then gauge the tenons centrally on the ends of the front and back rails (fig. 166). Cut the tenons and remove a ¼-in (6-mm) cover at the top and a ⅛-in (3-mm) cover at the bottom.

Mark the curve on the front and back rails by bending a thin lath of wood so that it drops by ¾ in (20 mm) at the center: Draw around this curve with a pencil. Cut out the curve.

Clean up the front and back rails and round off

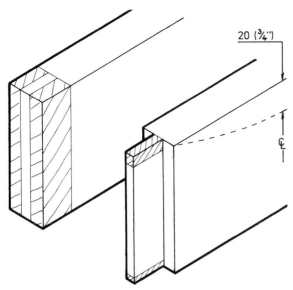

Fig. 166 *Gauge and cut the tenons on the front and back rails.*

the sharp edges on the underside, then polish these rails.

14) Gauge the tenons on the backrest ¼-in (6-mm) from the front (fig. 167). This will set the tenons

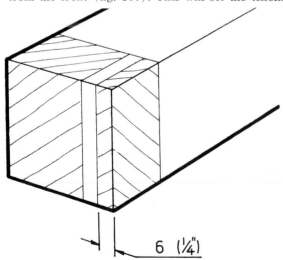

Fig. 167 *Gauge the tenons on the backrest.*

central when the rests have been later shaped to ¾ in (19 mm) thick. Bend a thin lath of wood to the curve of the backrests, and mark out the curve on the rests with a pencil. Your work will be stronger if you take into account any natural curve in the grain of the wood, and let this curve the same way as the rest rail.

Cut the tenons before you do the shaping, as then the wood is easier to hold in the vise. Note that the top rest will have a sloping haunch (fig. 168).

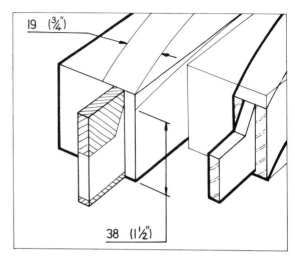

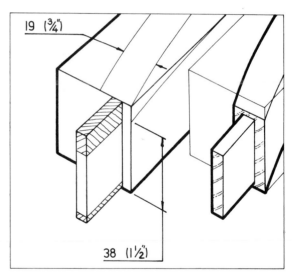

Fig. 168 *The top backrest has a sloping haunch.*

The backrests are curved in two ways: They are hollowed to fit your back, and they are curved lengthwise along the top edge. A good method of working seems to be:

a) Cut the inside curve, and clean it well.

b) Mark out and cut the curve on the top edge. Clean this curve properly.

c) Mark out and cut the curve on the back of the

rests so that the wood finishes ¾ in (19 mm) thick. This work can be done quite easily on a band-saw by setting the saw so that it follows the curve cut previously on the inside.

d) Clean up the back of the rests. Round off all sharp corners and polish all around.

15) Mark out the mortise positions on the inside of the side frames (fig. 169). Gauge the mortises for

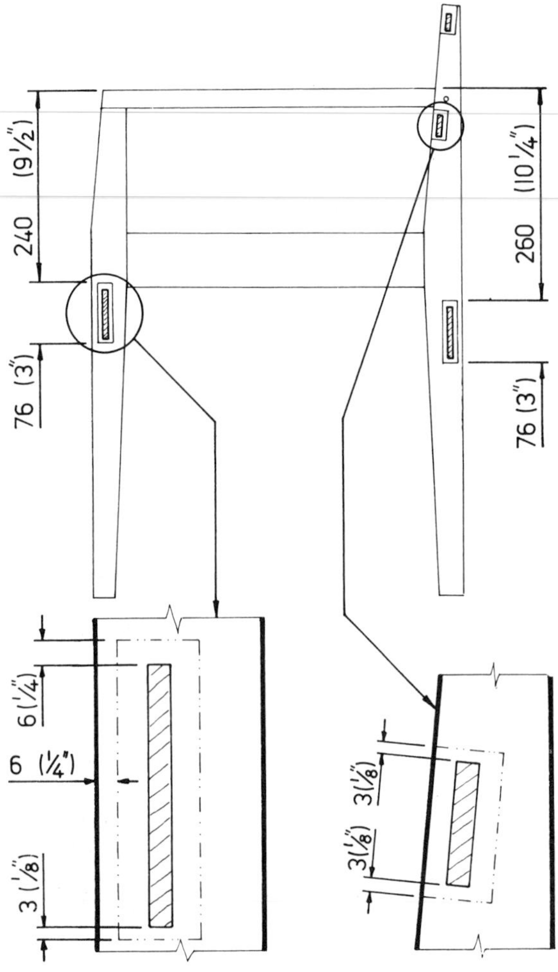

Fig. 169 *Mark out the mortise positions on the inside of the side frames.*

the front and back rails ⁹⁄₁₆ in (15 mm) from the edge—this will set the rails ¼ in (6 mm) in. The backrests will finish flush with the inside of the legs.

16) Chop the mortises ⅞ in (22 mm) deep.

17) Fit the joints and try the parts together without

glue. Clean up all the surfaces and round off sharp corners where it is possible. Cut the ends of the feet level. Polish the parts and then glue up. Do not apply too much pressure with the clamps, as it is easy to distort the curved backrest. Check carefully that the frame is true before leaving it for the glue to set.

18) Clean up the outside of the frame, and polish it.

THE SEAT

19) Cut the seat rails 17½ in (440 mm) long, then shape their top edges to the same curve as the front and back rails. Clean up the seat rails, then fix them into the chair using a 1¼-in (32-mm) screw through each end—let the seat rails stand clear of the front and back rails by an amount equal to the thickness of the covering material.

20) Trim the five pieces of plywood so they fit inside the chair with a ⅛-in (3-mm) gap between the outer edges of the seat and the frame of the chair. Note that it is an advantage to trim the edges of the plywood at an angle so that they meet each other correctly. Glue and screw the plywood to the

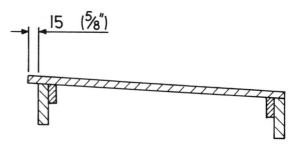

Fig. 170 *Glue and screw the plywood to the seat rails, allowing an overhang at the front seat rail.*

seat rails; allow a ⅝-in (15-mm) overhang at the front rail, but make a flush fit with the back rail (fig. 170).

21) When the glue has set, remove the seat from the frame by taking out the four 1¼-in (32-mm) screws.

THE UPHOLSTERY

22) Drill two ⅝-in (16-mm) diameter holes

through the plywood seat to allow for escape of air. Without these holes the plastic or leather covering might burst.

23) Use a rasp or coarse abrasive paper to round off all sharp corners and edges on the plywood seat. This process prevents the covering material from being cut through when the seat is used.

24) Fix a 1-in (25-mm) layer of dense chip foam to the plywood seat with a few dabs of contact adhesive. The excess foam can be removed with a bandsaw or sharp knife. Try to keep the edges of the foam vertical, and while the edges of the foam at the front and back can be kept level with the edges of the plywood seat, the edges of the foam at the sides should be left $\frac{1}{4}$ in (6 mm) full so as to press lightly against the frame of the chair.

25) Use a few dabs of contact adhesive to fix the 1-in (25-mm) layer of softer foam over the seat. In this case the sides are made flush with the reconstituted foam, but the front is brought over the edge and glued to the first $\frac{3}{8}$ in (10 mm) on the underside of the plywood, and the back is brought onto the edge of the plywood and fixed there with glue (fig. 171).

ing the material to an even shape and fixing as you go.

At the corners: Pull to the center of the corner and fix with one tack or staple, then pull and tuck

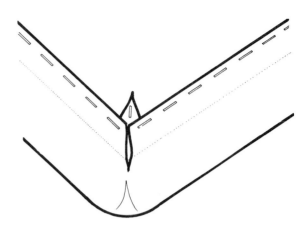

Fig. 172 Cut away the bulk of the upholstery material from under the tuck at the corner, and staple down.

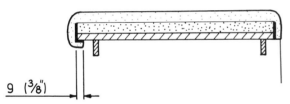

Fig. 171 Attach the medium-density foam to the top of the dense chip foam.

26) Measure the width of the seat accurately for the covering: Allow the material to go down the sides of the seat and onto the underside by about $1\frac{1}{4}$ in (32 mm). Cut the upholstery material to width.

27) Fix the upholstery material with either tacks or heavy-duty staples. Fix along the front edge first; then fix once in the middle of the back, and once in the middle of the two sides. Check the appearance of the seat, then work towards the corners by pull-

once at each side. Cut away the bulk of the material from under the tucks and staple down (fig. 172).

28) The buttons can be covered with $1\frac{1}{2}$-in (38-mm) diameter circles of upholstery material—some contact adhesive will help you fix the upholstery material to the button. Then drill four small holes through the plywood base of the seat. Use a very long upholstery needle to pass nylon thread right through the seat. Pass a loop of thread through a button on the top and a button on the underside of the seat, and tie off with a slip knot. Adjust the tension on the thread until the seat looks correct.

RECLINER

This chair looks difficult to make, but anyone who has some woodworking experience and patience to slip-stitch the upholstery cover onto the inner frame of the chair would be able to tackle its construction.

CUTTING LIST FOR RECLINER—planed, finished sizes

INNER FRAME:

Hardwood

key	description	quantity	length	width	thickness
A	back	2	27½ in (700 mm)	3½ in (90 mm)	1¼ in (32 mm)
B	seat	2	25½ in (650 mm)	5½ in (140 mm)	1¼ in (32 mm)
C	cross rails	3	18 in (460 mm)	2¼ in (58 mm)	1¼ in (32 mm)
D	top rail	1	18 in (460 mm)	6¾ in (170 mm)	1 in (25 mm)

Dowel

key	description	quantity	length	width	thickness
E		4	4 in (100 mm)	½-in (12-mm) diameter	

Medium-density upholstery foam

key	description	quantity	length	width	thickness
F	inside back	1	29 in (740 mm)	32 in (810 mm)	½ in (12 mm)
G	seat platform	1	23 in (590 mm)	15½ in (390 mm)	½ in (12 mm)
H	outside seat	2	27 in (690 mm)	9 in (230 mm)	½ in (12 mm)
I	front	1	19 in (480 mm)	10 in (250 mm)	½ in (12 mm)
J	seat cushion	1	19 in (480 mm)	20 in (510 mm)	4 in (100 mm)
K	back cushion	1	20 in (510 mm)	20 in (510 mm)	4 in (100 mm)
L	head cushion	1	8 in (200 mm)	20 in (510 mm)	4 in (100 mm)

Upholstery top cover

quantity	length	width
1	13 ft (4 m)	54 in (1,370 mm)

Hardware

16 ft (5 m) of 2-in (50-mm) wide rubber webbing
36 ⅝-in (15-mm) webbing tacks

OUTER FRAME:

Hardwood

key	description	quantity	length	width	thickness
M	floor rails	2	25½ in (650 mm)	2½ in (65 mm)	1⅜ in (35 mm)
N	uprights	4	20½ in (520 mm)	1¾ in (45 mm)	1⅛ in (29 mm)
O	arms	2	26½ in (670 mm)	2¾ in (70 mm)	1¼ in (32 mm)
P	cross rails	2	23 in (580 mm)	2⅜ in (20 mm)	1⅛ in (29 mm)

Hardware

6 steel flathead screws 2 in (50 mm) × no. 10
6 plastic screw caps

This chair (fig. 173) is both comfortable and very relaxing. The design consists of an inner frame that is made from hardwood, and which is fitted with rubber webbing. The inner frame is fully upholstered, and it supports three foam cushions that are upholstered with zip-off covers for their easy removal for dry cleaning. The inner frame is supported by a strong and attractive hardwood outer frame (fig. 174).

The original recliner chair was covered with mottled grey synthetic material, and had a mahogany outer frame.

CONSTRUCTION OF THE INNER FRAME

1) Use a pencil to mark out 1-in (25-mm) squares on the back and seat. Transfer the shapes onto these pieces (fig. 173).

2) Use either a coping saw or a machine bandsaw to cut out shape A accurately. Cut out shape B in such a way that a bar clamp can be used to hold the parts together until the glue has set.

3) Mark out the positions for the two dowels in each joint using the "pin" method. Drill the ½-in (12-mm) diameter holes over 2 in (50 mm) deep for the dowels: Some improvisation with a bench drill-stand and a bench vise can help you here.

4) Glue the joints thoroughly. Put them together and hold each with a bar clamp until the glue has set.

5) Complete the shaping of the glued-up sides: Hold the sides together in the vise and shape them identically, using a smoothing plane and spokeshave. The quality of the finish on these pieces is not important, but the shape should be smooth and pleasant.

6) Mark out the three cross rails and the top rail 17½ in (445 mm) long. Cut them to length.

7a) Glue the ends of the cross rails and the top rail, and place them in position between the frames. Hold the work together while the glue sets. I like to partially insert a few nails to stop the pieces from sliding around, and then I withdraw the nails later when the glue has set.

b) When the glue has set (i.e., the next day) drill two ⅜-in (9-mm) diameter holes 3 in (76 mm) deep through the side frames into the ends of all the rails. Glue and plug these holes with ⅜-in (9-mm)

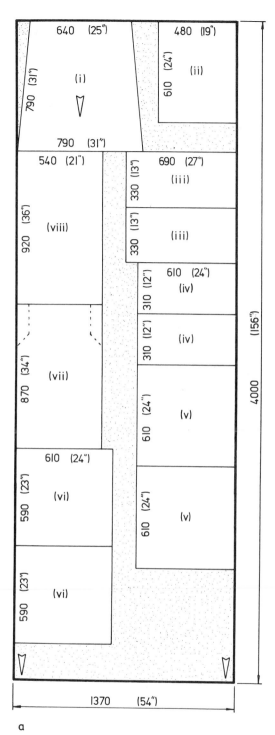

Fig. 173a Recliner chair: Cutting the upholstery cloth for: (i) inside back, (ii) seat platform, (iii) seat sides, (iv) head cushion, (v) back cushion, (vi) seat cushion, (vii) seat front, (viii) outside back.

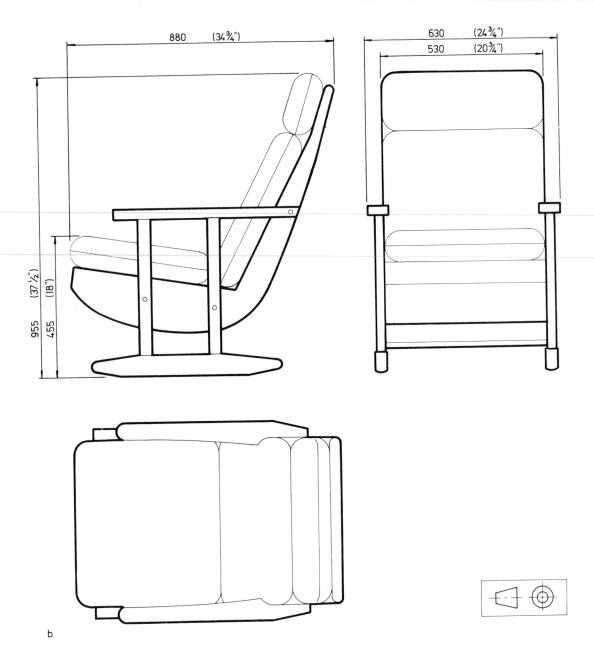

880   (34¾″)

630   (24¾″)

530   (20¾″)

955 (37½″)

455 (18″)

b

Fig. 173b Recliner chair: orthographic projection.

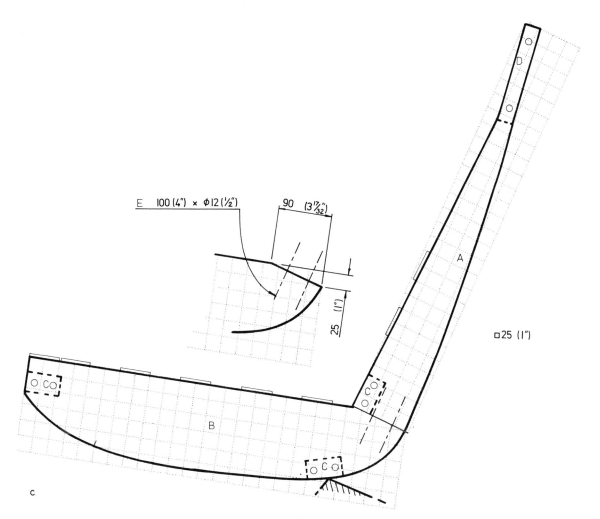

E   100 (4") × φ12 (½")

90   (3¹⁷/₃₂")

25 (1")

D

A

□25 (1")

B

C

Fig. 173c Recliner chair: The shape of the seat and back drawn over 1-in (25-mm) squares.

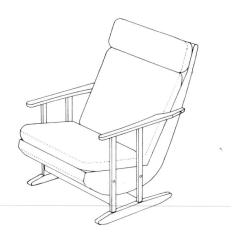

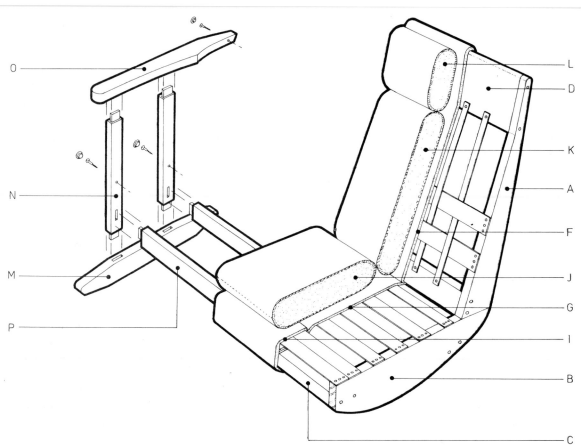

Fig. 174 Recliner chair: An exploded view of the construction.

dowels. This may seem a strange way to set about making a joint, but it is an effective method.

8) Plane the tops of the dowels flush with the surface of the wood, and trim any rails where necessary (i.e., the lowest rail needs slightly rounding over, and the top edge of the top rail also needs rounding).

THE UPHOLSTERY OF THE INNER FRAME

9) Round over all corners to about a ⅛-in (3-mm) radius with either a rasp or coarse abrasive paper. The purpose of rounding the edges is to prevent the upholstery materials from being cut through by the sharp edges on the frame.

10) Mark out two lengths of rubber webbing 17½ in (444 mm) long. Tack and stretch both of these across the front of the seat. An allowance has already been made for the amount of stretch required.

Mark out four more lengths of rubber webbing 18 in (457 mm) long and tack and stretch these at 2-in (50-mm) spaced intervals across the seat.

11) Mark out two lengths of rubber webbing 18 in (457 mm) long and tack these across the back for lumbar support. Now cut the rest of the webbing in half lengthwise and mark out four 19-in (483-mm) lengths for the back. Attach these to the back with one tack at each end; let the narrow webbing interlace with the wider webbing.

12) Fix the ½-in (12-mm) foam on the inside of the back with a few dabs of contact adhesive. Wrap the foam around the edge and onto the back of the frame: Trim off any excess with scissors.

Tear a piece of calico 32 in (810 mm) × 32 in (810 mm). Mark the centers top and bottom, then fix the calico to the underside of the back rail working from the center outwards—a 1-in (25-mm) slit in the calico will allow it to go around the edges of the back. Fix the calico along the back of the top rail, then attach the edges onto the back of the frame. Of course, the fixing is carried out either with ⅜-in (9-mm) tacks or with staples. Trim off the excess calico.

13) Pad the outside of the top rail with pieces of ½-in (12-mm) foam to make up a piece 18 in (460 mm) × 6 in (150 mm) × ½ in (12 mm).

Tear a piece of calico 36 in (920 mm) × 20 in (510 mm). Turn the edges in, and staple a) along the outside of the top rail to cover the foam b) and

c) down the edges of the frame as far as the bend, leaving the bottom flap open until a later stage.

14a) Upholster the inside of the back with top cover material (fig. 174): Stuff a little wadding under the top edge and into the top corners as you work.

b) Upholster the outside of the back: Back-tack along the top edge through a ½-in (12-mm) strip of cardboard (fig. 175) and pin or partially staple

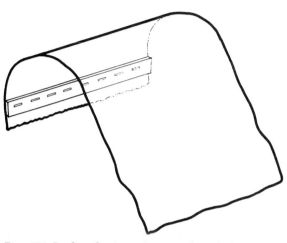

Fig. 175 Back-tack along the top edge of the upholstery material with a narrow strip of cardboard.

along the edges as far as the bend in the frame; then slip-stitch down these edges, making stitches at ⅜-in (9-mm) intervals with a curved needle and pulling out the pins or staples as you work.

15) Cover the outsides of the seat with ½-in (12-mm) thick foam. Glue the foam to the top and bottom edges of the sides and trim away any excess foam. Cover the foam with calico, using ⅜-in (9-mm) tacks or staples to fix the calico.

16) Now make a sandwich for the seat platform: Use the ½-in (12-mm) thick foam, a piece of calico 24 in (610 mm) × 19 in (480 mm), and a piece of top cover material 24 in (610 mm) × 19 in (480 mm). Turn the top cover in and hem along the long edges—this will prevent fraying.

Lay this sandwich over the four webbings on the seat, and tack off along the underside of the back rail. Pass the sandwich under the two front webs and tack off along the front rail (fig. 176): Do not stretch the material.

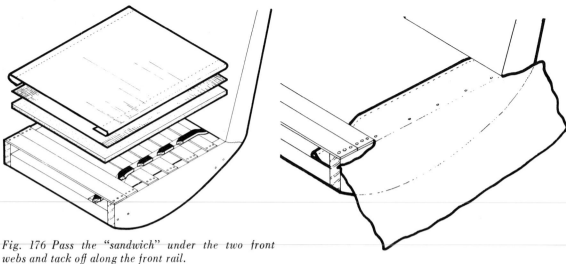

Fig. 176 Pass the "sandwich" under the two front webs and tack off along the front rail.

17) Upholster the sides of the seat. Take the two pieces of top cover material for the seat sides and note the direction of the pile: Hem the long edge so that the pile brushes away from this hem.

Lightly tack the top cover to the top edge of the seat rail (fig. 177, a) so that the material overlaps the seat platform. Now back-tack through a ½-in (12-mm) strip of cardboard (fig. 177, b). Apply some wadding over the back-tacking, then pull the top cover over the wadding and down the sides and tack off along the under-edge of the side rail (fig. 177, c).

Fit the cover around the back corner of the frame—cut some of the bulk of the covering material away, but take care not to take too much away or the frame will show.

At the front corner: Cut against the back-tacking for a distance of 4 in (100 mm). Tuck this piece under the two front webs, and tack off on the front rail. Now neaten off the corners where necessary.

18) Tack a piece of calico along the front rail, along the sides, and onto the bottom rail—this covers the bottom of the chair entirely.

19) Glue a piece of ½-in (12-mm) foam to the top of both of the front webs: Take care not to get glue on your upholstery work!

Place a piece of wadding over the foam to separate the foam from the top cover material. Tack the

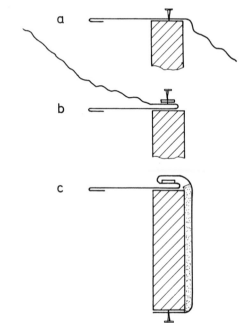

Fig. 177 Upholster the sides of the seat: (a) tack the top cover to the edge of the seat rail (b), & (c) back-tack through cardboard and add wadding.

top cover, upside down, onto the front rail underneath the web (fig. 178, a). Bring the top cover over the webbing and temporarily tack it down along the edges. Slip-stitch along the edges, then remove the temporary tacks (fig. 178, b). This should complete the upholstery work.

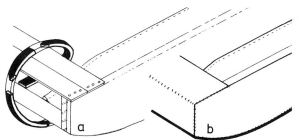

Fig. 178 Tack the top cover upside-down onto the front rail underneath the webs.

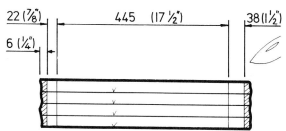

Fig. 180 Hold the four uprights together and mark out with a knife.

CONSTRUCTION OF THE OUTER FRAME

20) Choose the best surfaces on all the pieces of wood and mark these in pencil with face-side and face-edge marks.

21) Hold the floor rails together, mark them to length (fig. 179), and mark out the mortise positions in pencil.

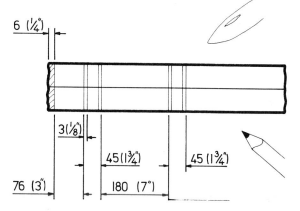

Fig. 181 Mark out the mortise limit lines on the arms with a pencil.

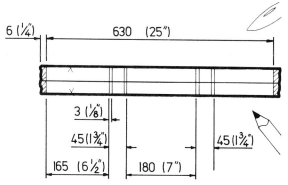

Fig. 179 Hold the floor rails together and mark them to length.

22) Hold the four uprights together and mark out with a knife (fig. 180). Separate the uprights, and square the knife lines around each piece.

23) Place both of the arms together face-side downwards. Mark only the front of the arms with a knife—the overall length can be ascertained later at the fitting stage. Mark out the mortise limit lines in pencil (fig. 181).

24) Set the spurs on a mortise gauge to the width

of the $\frac{1}{4}$-in (6-mm) mortise chisel. Then (fig. 182, a) set the stock of the gauge so that the mortises can be marked centrally in the floor rails. Gauge also the mortises in the underside of the arms working from the outside edge (fig. 182, b). Reset the stock of the gauge and gauge the tenons centrally around both ends of the uprights (fig. 182, c). Hatch in the waste.

25) Chop the mortises $1\frac{5}{8}$ in (42 mm) deep in the floor rails. Chop the mortises 1 in (25 mm) deep in the arms. Saw the tenons and remove $\frac{1}{8}$ in (3 mm) from the edges of the tenons as "covers" in order to conceal the mortises.

26) Fit all joints and number them consecutively A-A, B-B, etc.

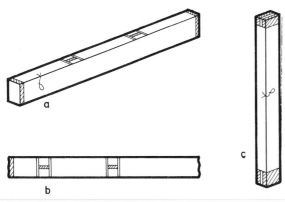

Fig. 182 Gauging: (a) the mortises centrally in the floor rails, (b) the mortises in the underside of the arms, (c) the tenons at both ends of the uprights.

27) Hold the two front uprights together face-side downwards, and mark out the mortise positions for the cross rail (fig. 183).

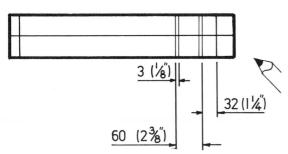

Fig. 183 Holding the two front uprights together, mark out the mortise positions for the cross rail.

28) Hold the two back uprights together face-side downwards, and mark out the mortise positions for the cross rail (fig. 184).

29) Gauge the ¼-in (6-mm) mortises centrally on the uprights, and chop these mortises ⅞ in (22 mm) deep.

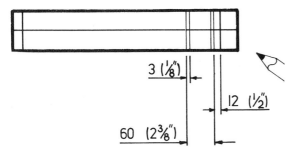

Fig. 184 Holding the two back uprights together, mark out the mortise positions for the cross rail.

30) Hold the cross rails together and mark out the rabbet lines for the joints with a knife (fig. 185). Note: The distance shown here as 21 in (533 mm) should be checked against the upholstered frame—there is no need to press hard against the upholstery when taking this measurement. Separate the cross rails, and square the knife lines around each rail.

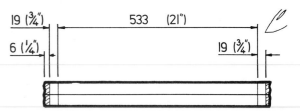

Fig. 185 Hold the cross rails together and mark out the rabbet lines for the joints with a knife.

31) Cut the waste from the ends of the cross rails. Gauge the ¼-in (6-mm) tenons centrally around each rail, then cut the tenons in the normal way. Remove ⅛ in (3 mm) from each side of the tenons for a cover. Fit the joints together.

32) Shape the pieces as follows:

a) Mark out the shaping on the sides of the floor rails in pencil (fig. 186). Saw to within ⅛ in (3 mm) of the lines, then trim back to the lines using a smoothing plane or spokeshave.

b) Shape the bottom edge of both floor rails so that the chair can be slid easily over a carpeted floor (fig. 187).

c) Mark out the shaping with a pencil on the top of the arm (fig. 188). The chair should be loosely assembled, and the marking-out checked before any attempt is made to carry out the work.

33) Clean up all surfaces by removing one or two shavings with a finely set smoothing plane. Round over all sharp corners wherever possible. I prefer to polish the parts at this stage before they are glued together.

34) Glue the side frames. Then, when the glue has set, glue the cross rails into the side frames.

35) Attach the outer frame to the inner frame with six steel flathead screws 2 in (50 mm) × no. 10. The heads of the screws can be covered with plastic caps. You may find it necessary to reduce the diameter of the heads of the screws with a file if the screw caps are to cover the screw holes.

36) The head cushion can be attached to the frame

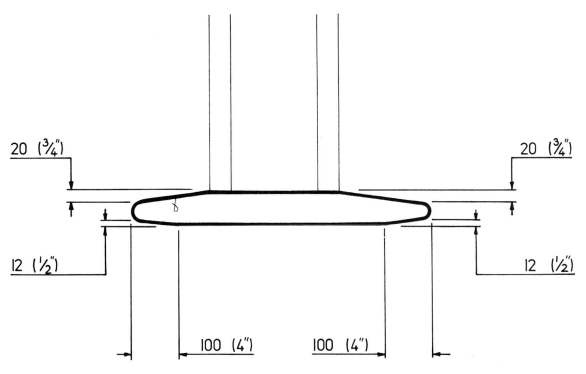

20 (¾")　　　　　　　　　　　　　　　　20 (¾")

12 (½")　　　　　　　　　　　　　　　　12 (½")

100 (4")　　100 (4")

Fig. 186 Mark out the shaping on the sides of the floor rails with a pencil.

Fig. 187 Shape the bottom edge of the floor rails so that the chair will slide easily over a carpeted floor.

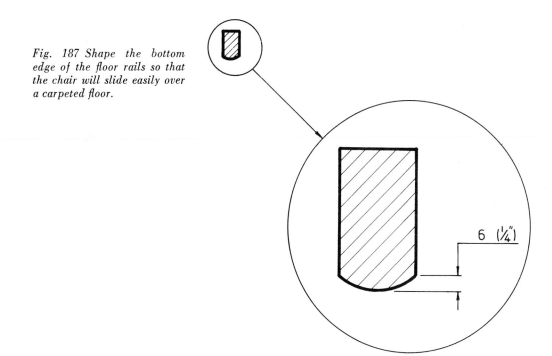

6 (¼")

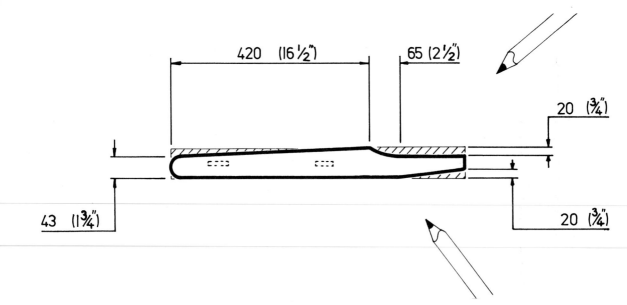

420 (16 ½")   65 (2 ½")   20 (¾")

43 (1¾")   20 (¾")

Fig. 188 Mark out the shaping on the top of the arm with a pencil.

with two carpet studs. It was found that the cushions looked better when wrapped with Da-cron™ and then covered with the upholstery material.

SIDEBOARD

Here is a sideboard that is small enough to fit easily into a modern home (fig. 189). The carcass is constructed with hand-cut dovetail joints, which are a decorative feature of this sideboard. The doors (fig. 190) are built as frames, which then have tongue-and-groove strips of wood glued on top: The strips are further secured by decorative wooden pegs. Piano hinges are used to hang the doors.

Inside the cabinet (fig. 191) there is one central division: The shelves on either side of the division are adjustable in height. The back of the cabinet is made from a panel of fibreboard (hardboard) that is covered with burlap (wall hessian): This reduces the weight of the sideboard, simplifies the construction, and has an attractive appearance.

The sideboard is not suitable for construction by a beginner, but anyone with some woodworking knowledge should be able to tackle it. The original sideboard was made from Iroko, and soon after construction turned from its original yellow to a rich golden brown.

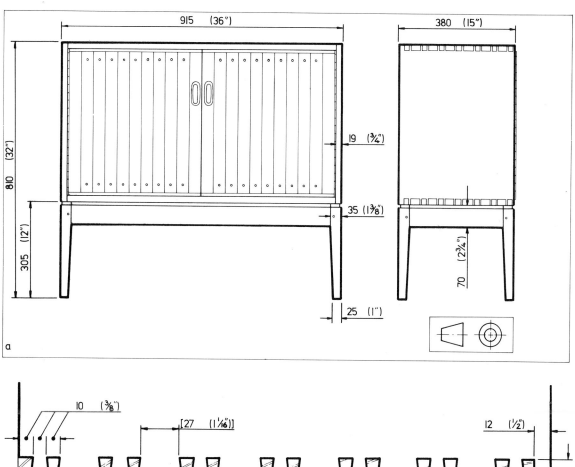

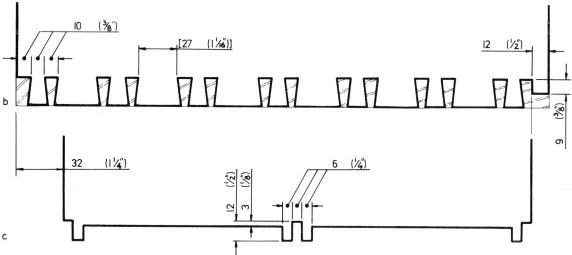

Fig. 189 Sideboard: (*a*) *orthographic projection,* (*b*) *dovetail arrangement,* (*c*) *the arrangement for the mortise-and-tenon with dado.*

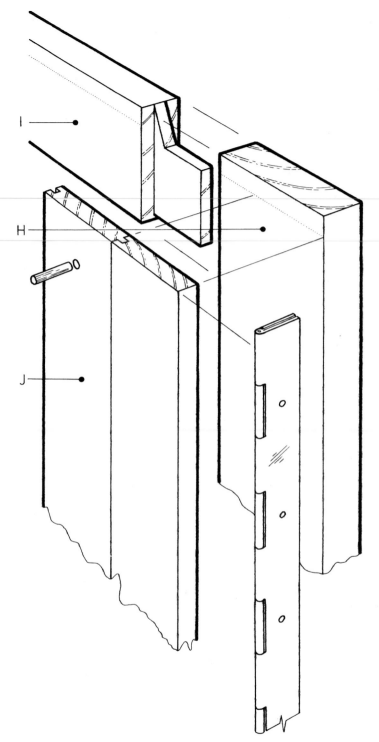

Fig. 190 *An exploded view of the door construction.*

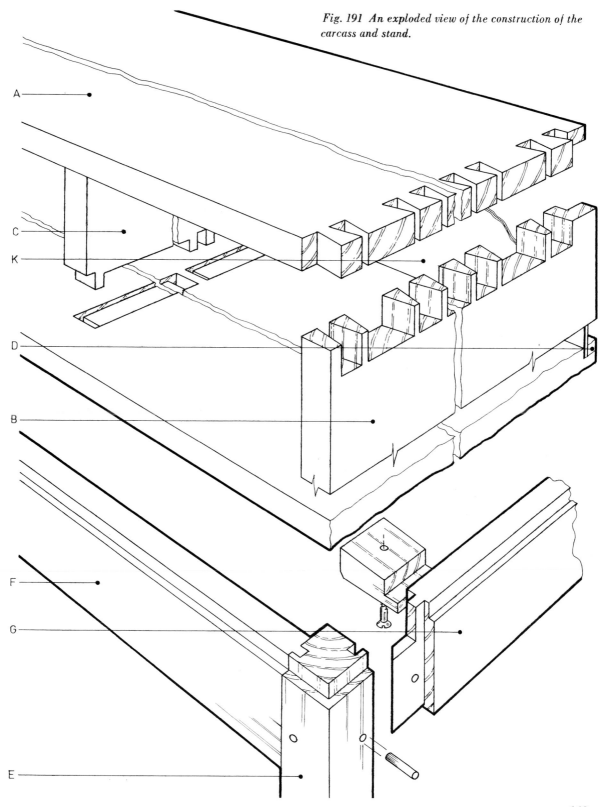

A

C

K

D

B

F

G

E

CUTTING LIST FOR SIDEBOARD

Hardwood

key	description	quantity	length	width	thickness
	CARCASS:				
A	top & bottom	2	36½ in (930 mm)	15 in (380 mm)	¾ in (19 mm)
B	ends	2	20½ in (520 mm)	15 in (380 mm)	¾ in (19 mm)
C	division	1	20½ in (520 mm)	13¼ in (340 mm)	¾ in (19 mm)
D	back strips	2	36 in (920 mm)	⅜ in (10 mm)	¼ in (6 mm)
	back strips	2	20 in (500 mm)	⅜ in (10 mm)	¼ in (6 mm)
	STAND:				
E	legs	4	12½ in (320 mm)	1⅜ in (35 mm)	1⅜ in (35 mm)
F	long rails	2	36 in (920 mm)	2¾ in (70 mm)	⅞ in (22 mm)
G	short rails	2	20 in (500 mm)	2¾ in (70 mm)	⅞ in (22 mm)
	DOORS:				
H	stiles	4	19 in (480 mm)	2½ in (63 mm)	¾ in (19 mm)
I	rails	4	16 in (400 mm)	2½ in (63 mm)	¾ in (19 mm)
J	panels	22	19 in (480 mm)	1⅞ in (48 mm)	⅜ in (10 mm)

Fibreboard (hardboard)

key	description	quantity	length	width	thickness
K	back	1	36 in (900 mm)	20 in (500 mm)	⅛ in (3 mm)

Hardware

2 brass piano hinges 19 in (480 mm) × ¾ in (19 mm)
⅝-in (16-mm) brass flathead screws for piano hinges
2 magnetic catches with screws
12 brass flathead screws 1¼ in (32 mm) × no. 8
20 brass flathead screws ½ in (12 mm) × no. 2

Burlap (wall hessian)

2 pieces 36 in (900 mm) × 20 in (500 mm)

CARCASS

1) Select the best grain for the top, and try to match the grain in the sides. Number the front corners on the outside (fig. 192).

2) Mark the top and bottom to a length of 36 in (915 mm). Cut the waste from the ends with a saw, then plane the pieces accurately to length. Similarly, finish the sides 20 in (510 mm) long.

3) Set a cutting gauge to $\frac{1}{16}$ in (2 mm) greater than the thickness of the wood, and lightly gauge a line around each end on all four pieces of wood. This line is called the rabbet line of the joint.

Copy the drawing of the dovetail joint (fig. 189)

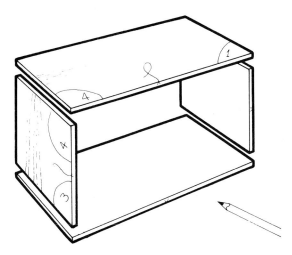

Fig. 192 *Number the front corners of the carcass in sequence with a pencil.*

full size on a piece of paper, and then transfer the measurements onto the rabbet line on the outside of just the carcass top and bottom: Use a pencil for this and take care to reverse the drawing so that the rabbet remains at the back of the cabinet.

With a dovetail template (fig. 193) draw in the complete dovetail shapes using a pencil, and hatch in the waste between the tails.

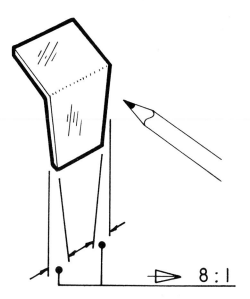

Fig. 193 *A dovetail template is used to mark out the correct angle of the dovetail.*

4) Cut the dovetails (*see* figs. 51–56). Do not cut the pins at the back, as these will be trimmed later to conceal the rabbet—the joints cannot be tried together at this stage.

5) Shape the rabbet for the back $\frac{3}{8}$ in (9 mm) $\times$ $\frac{1}{2}$ in (12 mm). Trim the back pins to fit the rabbet. Then tap the joints together without glue by using a hammer on a block of wood.

6) Square one end of the division with a plane. Use a cutting gauge to mark the rabbet line for a joint $\frac{1}{2}$ in (12 mm) from this end. Mark a second rabbet line the correct distance away from the first rabbet line—this distance can be found from the carcass ends—and allow $\frac{1}{2}$ in (12 mm) for the joint. Saw off the waste.

With a mortise gauge mark out the tenons and the dado (figs. 189 & 191).

7) Cut the tenons, the mortises, and the dado (*see* figs. 46–50).

8) Fit the joints on the division.

Then take the carcass apart and clean up all the inside surfaces—do this by removing one or two shavings with a finely set smoothing plane. Polish the inside surfaces.

9) Glue the carcass together. Work quickly, since the carcass must be put together before the glue sets. Several bar clamps are required to hold the work while the glue sets. Check that the carcass is square by measuring the diagonals at the front and back to see they are the same—give the carcass a push on one corner to square it up if it is required.

When the glue has set, the outside can be cleaned up and polished.

10) Cut the fibreboard (hardboard) back to fit into the rabbet. Glue burlap (wall hessian) onto both sides of the back using the appropriate adhesive—such as *Clam 143*.

The back is retained in the rabbet by hardwood strips. The strips are mitered at the corners, and fastened at intervals by $\frac{1}{2}$-in (12-mm) $\times$ no. 2 brass screws (fig. 194).

THE STAND

11) Select the best grain for the outside of the legs and rails, and mark the outside surfaces in pencil with face-side and face-edge marks.

12) Put the legs together face-side downwards, and

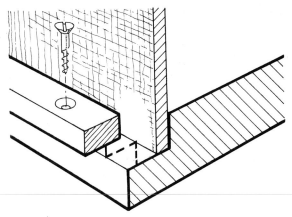

Fig. 194 A cross-sectional look through the rear of the carcass shows how the back is fixed in position.

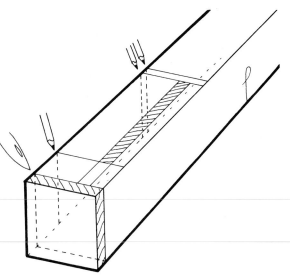

Fig. 196 Square the lines around the legs.

hold them in the vise. Mark out the overall length of 12 in (305 mm) with a marking knife to mark the lines (fig. 195). Use a pencil to transfer the width of a rail onto the legs, and to mark the mortise limit as well as the extent of the haunch.

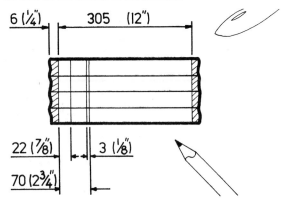

Fig. 195 Mark out the legs.

Square the knife lines around each leg, but square the pencil lines onto one other surface only—this surface must not be the face-side or face-edge (fig. 196).

Set the spurs on the mortise gauge to the width apart of the ¼-in (6-mm) mortise chisel. Set the gauge so that the spurs are in a central position on the edge of a rail. Then use the gauge to mark in the mortises, working either from the face-side or the face-edge of each leg.

13) Chop the mortises to meet one another inside each leg—this is a depth of about 1¹⁄₁₆ in (27 mm) (*see* fig. 39).

14) Place the long rails in the vise, and on the edge of them mark out the knife lines shown in fig. 197. Check that the distance between the tenons when added to the thickness of the leg will result in the stand being the correct overall length for the carcass. Square the knife lines around each piece and saw the waste from the ends.

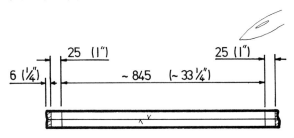

Fig. 197 Mark out the long rails.

Similarly mark out and cut to length the end rails (fig. 198).

Use the mortise gauge set as it was for marking the mortises, and gauge the position of the tenons (fig. 199). Hatch in the waste with a pencil.

15) Cut the tenons (*see* figs. 40 & 41). The ends of the tenons have to be mitered, to avoid them touching one another (fig. 191).

16) The stand will be fastened to the carcass by wooden buttons. Four buttons are needed on each long side and two buttons on each end. Slots ⅜ in (10 mm) deep are cut for the buttons on the inside of the rails (fig. 200).

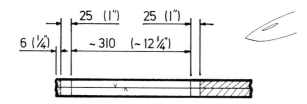

Fig. 198 Mark out the end rails.

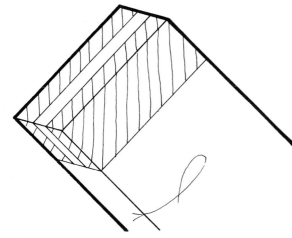

Fig. 199 Gauge the tenons on the rails and hatch in the waste.

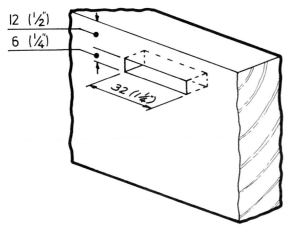

Fig. 200 Button slots have to be cut ⅜ in (10 mm) deep into the rails.

17) Plane a taper on the inside of the leg from below the joint to the foot. The foot finishes 1 in (25 mm) square.

Clean up the inside surfaces, polish these surfaces, and glue the stand together.

18) Hardwood pegs can be made to strengthen the joint and to improve the appearance, by splitting the wood with a chisel into pieces just bigger than ¼ in (6 mm) × ¼ in (6 mm) × 1 in (25 mm) long. The pieces are driven with a hammer through a hole in a steel plate—this makes the pieces round. To do this effectively the hole in the plate should be deeply countersunk, and the plate placed over a hole in the bench when the pegs are driven through.

19) A small rabbet is worked around the top of the stand to conceal any discrepancy in size between the stand and the carcass (fig. 201). The rabbet also improves the finished appearance. Then clean up and polish the outside surfaces.

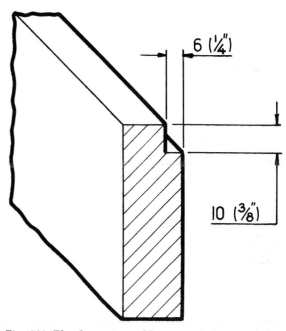

Fig. 201 The decorative rabbet around the top of the stand.

20) Make hardwood buttons (fig. 202), and fix the stand to the carcass with 1¼-in (32-mm) screws.

DOORS

21) Mark a face-side and face-edge on each piece. Place the stiles against the carcass and mark each stile to length; allow a trifle more than this so that the doors can be trimmed after completion, and square the lines around each end.

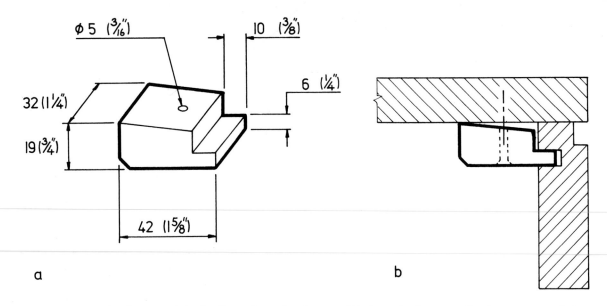

a

b

Fig. 202 *Wooden buttons:* (a) *the dimensions of a button,* (b) *how the button pulls the carcass and the stand together.*

Use a pencil to transfer the width of a rail to the stile, and to mark the mortise limit line, as well as the extent of the haunch (fig. 203).

Set the spurs on the mortise gauge to the width apart of the ¼-in (6-mm) mortise chisel. Then set the gauge to mark centrally on the edge of the stile. Gauge the mortise and haunch from the face side. Hatch in the mortise with a pencil (fig. 204).

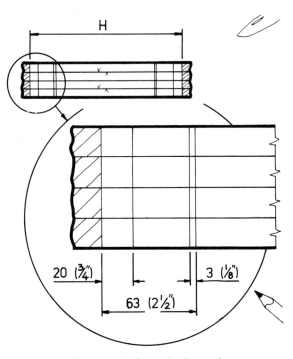

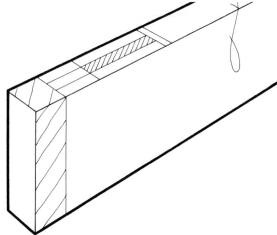

Fig. 204 *The mortise and haunch marked-out on the stiles.*

22) Chop the mortises 1⅜ in (35 mm) deep (*see* fig. 39).

23) Place the stiles against the carcass and measure the rabbet length for the rails: Allow a trifle more, and mark this centrally on the rails. Mark out the lines for the ends of the tenons (fig. 205).

Fig. 203 *Mark out the door stiles.*

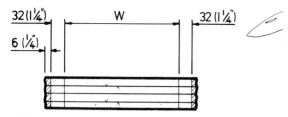

Fig. 205 Mark out the door rails.

Saw the waste from the ends of the rails; then, with the mortise gauge set as it was for marking the mortises, gauge the tenons from the face side. Hatch in the waste (fig. 206).

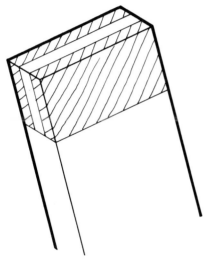

Fig. 206 Gauge the tenons on the ends of the door rails.

24) Cut the tenons (see figs. 40 & 41).

25) Fit the joints. Clean up and polish the inside edges. Glue up each door using two bar clamps to hold the work. Make sure each door is square by measuring the diagonals and seeing they are the same, and check that each door is flat before leaving for the glue to dry.

26) Plane the sides of each door flat. Then fit the doors in their final position by planing the hinge edge true, planing the bottom edge to line up with the carcass, then planing the top edge so the door fits the carcass. Allow a slight clearance so that the door does not bind.

27) Arrange the panels for matching color and grain, then tongue-and-groove the pieces—some thought is required here if the pieces are to appear the same width when in position. A small space is required between the strips to allow them to expand should they need to do so.

Clean up the backs of the panels, then cut them $\frac{3}{8}$ in (9 mm) shorter than the frames at the top and the bottom. Clean up the ends of the panels.

28) Glue the outer strips on the panels to the frames and put a small dab of glue behind each of the other strips—do not glue the tongues or grooves. Clamp the panels tightly to the frames until the glue has set. Afterwards, the strips can be drilled and pegged in place.

29) Rabbet the doors for the hinges, then clean up and polish the doors.

Fix the hinges with two screws, and try the doors to see that they work before you put in the remainder of the screws. Plane the handle edge on each door at a slight angle so the doors clear one another. Each door can be retained in the closed position by a magnetic catch.

What Next?

By now, you have most likely made several pieces of furniture using ideas from this book, and have probably created other items not described here that are needed in your home. The next likely question is: What can you do to develop your skills? Here are a number of possibilities drawn from my own experience.

CRAFT SOCIETIES

A craft society is a welcome alternative for the craftsman who gets lonely while working by himself at home. A good craft society will bring together within a geographical region people who actively participate in different crafts. Members of a crafts society might include glass blowers, jewellers, potters, weavers, woodturners, and furniture-makers. For some of these members their craft is a hobby, for many it is a part-time occupation, and for a few it is a full-time occupation.

The craft society to which I belong has two forms of membership: These we called associated and full. A full member has to pay a higher annual fee than an associate member, but the full member can vote at the Annual General Meeting, can be elected to the committee which runs the day-to-day affairs of the society, and has the right to sell pieces of work through the annual exhibition. It is not easy to become a full member of this society: Usually three pieces of your work have to be submitted for scrutiny by the committee, and some people do get turned away.

Very briefly, the aims of a craft society are usually:
* to promote the crafts movement
* to provide a newsletter for the members
* to help overcome the feeling of isolation by providing slide shows, visits to members' workshops, etc.
* to provide a crafts weekend that is usually made to coincide with the Annual General Meeting. Dur-

ing this weekend, members can speak with visiting craftspeople.
* to organize an annual exhibition as a shop window and as a selling place.

RESOURCE CENTERS

Many of us had the opportunity of studying craft subjects while we attended school; however, upon reaching adult life we no longer have resources available to us. To set up a workshop at home that is as comprehensively equipped as the workshops in many schools would be not only expensive, but also in a sense wasteful of resources. I suggest, therefore, that resource centers be created where members can go to use the equipment. Presumably, people who practice other crafts may be interested in the same idea, but thinking initially of woodworkers I would like to see a bandsaw, a circular saw, a drilling machine, a machine planer and a woodturning lathe made available.

The resource center may require a permanent technician to maintain the equipment and to ensure that the machines are used properly. The cost of this service need not be exorbitant. Indeed, the center could be self-financing—rather like a golf club—with members paying a membership fee and a fee for every visit made. The center would be open to all, for the more people use it, the more successful it will be.

SELLING YOUR WORK

Not everyone wishes to sell the furniture they have made. Certainly some of the articles I have designed and made have felt so much a part of me that I have not wanted to part with them.

"How much do you sell a picture for?" I once asked an artist friend, and he replied that everything had its price and it was just a question of how much money he required before he became willing to part with his work. As far as I can see, there are two reasons why you may wish to sell your work: First, you need the money; second, you need the space if you are to continue to make other articles. In the first instance you will have to price your time into the cost of the article, but in the second instance where you enjoy making furniture then the lowest price you ask is the cost of the materials.

People who sell articles are mentally in a rather different position from myself. I like to solve problems and play with new ideas, whereas people who sell their work rely heavily upon repeating ideas. The idea of constant repetition does not appeal to me; if many things of the same kind have to be made, then the machine is the better answer to the problem.

I know of people who sell directly to stores. These people live in a prime tourist area, so they find a ready market. I know of someone who makes and sells three-legged stools, small coffee tables, wooden toys, and the occasional rocking chair: The smaller and less-expensive articles are always the easiest to sell.

If you do wish to sell your work, then here are five suggestions for obtaining markets:

1) Join a crafts society with the object of selling your work through the annual exhibition. If you cannot find a crafts society in your area, form one with friends who have craft interests.

2) Show samples of your work to stores.

3) Advertise in the local newspaper.

4) Tell the people in the vicinity of your place of work about your hobby. I have had several colleagues ask me to make things for them. One lady has come to me three Christmases running asking me to make toys for her children.

If in time you think seriously about going into business on a full-time basis, then you may need some business advice.

COURSES

There are only a few short courses offered in furniture making. Most of the courses that are available are advertised in the craft magazines.

TEACHING AS A CAREER

You could take up teaching as a career, but to do so you would not only have to like woodworking, but you would have to like teaching and working with children. You should also recognize that the children are a captive audience, so they are not all going to be as interested in woodworking as you are. In addition, there are pressures upon you. There are the expectations of the pupils, the parents, the headmaster, and the advisory staff; unfortunately, these expectations are not always the same.

An alternative to a secondary school is teaching at a technical college. There you would work with older students who have chosen to study your subject. You may, however, be expected to have had some industrial experience before being given a full-time post.

A third possibility would be to teach at an adult institute. There you would be working with interested adults. Much of your teaching would be done during the evenings, but it is doubtful whether you would find sufficient work to be able to be employed full-time.

There is a fourth possibility of working with handicapped people. Teaching handicapped people can initially be very difficult, but becomes easier and very rewarding.

APPENDICES

Appendix A

TOOL KIT CHECKLIST

woodwork bench with vise
backsaw—10-in (250-mm) blade
coping saw with spare blades
small-bladed penknife, or marking knife
stainless steel ruler—12 in (300 mm) long
try square—6-in (150-mm) blade
marking gauge
mortise gauge
hand drill
high speed drills—$\frac{1}{16}$ in (1.5 mm) to $\frac{1}{4}$ in (6 mm)
countersink bit
screwdrivers—assorted sizes
hammer—14 oz (400 g)

C clamp (G cramp)—6-in (150-mm) capacity
two bar clamps or clamp heads—42 in (1.070 m) bar
cork block
plow plane
bevelled-edge chisel—$\frac{1}{4}$ in (6 mm)
mortise chisel—$\frac{1}{4}$ in (6 mm)
firmer chisel—$1\frac{1}{4}$ in (32 mm)
mallet
Norton India medium-grade oilstone—8 in (200 mm) $\times$ 2 in (50 mm) $\times$ 1 in (25 mm)
can of light-grade machine oil

Appendix B

This is a shortened world list of woods and should be adequate wherever you live in the world. The weight that is given for each species is the approximate weight for an air-dried sample. NOTE: Species marked with an asterisk* are a potential health hazard when worked using machines that have not been fitted with an efficient dust extraction system.

SOME SUITABLE SOFTWOODS

COMMON NAME	BOTANICAL NAME	ORIGIN	WEIGHT LB/FT³ (KG/M³)	COLOR	COMMENT
1) Douglas Fir or Columbian Pine	*Pseudotsuga taxifolia*	British Columbia	33 (530)	Red to brown background with prominent growth rings	This has an attractive appearance. It is usually straight-grained and knot-free, and is used for ladder construction and for gymnasium apparatus.
2) Pine, Cypress	*Cupressus*	Australia	42 (670)	Yellowish brown	This wood is decorative with dark streaks, and it has an aromatic camphor-like smell.
3) Pine, Parana	*Araucaria angustifolia*	South America	34 (540)	Straw to dark brown with bright red streaks	Parana pine is straight-grained, usually knot-free, and takes paint and varnish well.
4) Pine, Pitch	*Pinus caribaea*	USA	41 (660)	Yellowish brown background with prominent growth rings	Pitch pine is straight-grained, has a coarse uniform texture, and is resinous.
5) Pine, Yellow or White Pine	*Pinus strobus*	Eastern Canada and USA	26 (420)	Light yellow to reddish brown	This wood is straight-grained with indistinct growth rings. It has a medium-coarse, even texture and is mildly resinous.

Name	Botanical name	Origin	Density	Colour	Description
6) Redwood or Scots Pine or Red Deal	*Pinus sylvestris*	Russia, Baltic and Canada	34 (540)	Reddish to yellowish brown	This softwood is moderately resinous and fairly straight-grained. It has good strength properties and is a popular building material.
7) Rimu	*Dacrydium cupressinum*	New Zealand	37 (590)	Yellow-brown to reddish brown	Rimu is an attractive softwood with dark streaks. It is a popular building material.
8) Spruce, Eastern or White Spruce	*Picea engelmannii*	Eastern Canada and USA	26 (420)	Pale yellow-brown, almost white	This wood is in all respects like Whitewood.
9) Spruce, Sitka	*Picea sitchensis*	British Columbia, Western USA	27 (440)	Light pinkish brown	Sitka spruce can grow to a very large tree. The wood is used for making planes, masts, oars, and musical instruments.
10) Western Hemlock	*Tsuga haterophylla*	Canada and Northwest USA	30 (480)	Pale yellow-brown with red tinge	Western Hemlock has a straight grain and a moderately fine texture.
11) *Western Red Cedar	*Thuja plicata*	Canada and Northwest USA	25 (400)	Reddish brown	This is a soft wood with a distinctive fragrance. It is naturally resistant to decay and is used for unpainted exterior work.

SOME SUITABLE SOFTWOODS

COMMON NAME	BOTANICAL NAME	ORIGIN	WEIGHT LB/FT³ (KG/M³)	COLOR	COMMENT
12) White-wood or European Spruce	*Picea abies*	Russia, Baltic, Canada	26 (420)	Light yellowish brown, almost white	This is the European Christmas tree. The wood is straight grained, mildly lustrous, and has a fairly even texture. It is a popular building material, and is sometimes used for making kitchen cabinets.

SOME SUITABLE HARDWOODS

COMMON NAME	BOTANICAL NAME	ORIGIN	WEIGHT LB/FT³ (KG/M³)	COLOR	COMMENT
1) Albarco or Red Jetquitiba	*Cariniana legalis*	Colombia and Brazil	36 (580)	Pinkish to reddish brown	This wood is straight-grained. It has a medium texture and a fairly uniform color.
2) Abura	*Mitragyna stipulosa*	West Africa	36 (580)	Light brown to pinkish	Abura is fairly straight-grained, has an even texture, and works well. It takes a good finish, but generally lacks character.

	Name	Botanical name	Origin	Weight	Color	Description
3)	Afrormosia or Kokrodua	*Afrormosia elata*	West Africa	44 (710)	Warm honey toning to brownish yellow with darker streaks	This wood is very stable and is sometimes regarded as a substitute for Teak, but it has a finer texture than Teak and it does not have an oily nature.
4)	Agba or Tola	*Cossweilerodendron balsamiferum*	West Africa	35 (560)	Pale yellow straw color	This wood is straight-grained, has a fairly close, even texture, and works well. It has a distinctive mild peppery smell.
5)	Beech, European	*Fagus sylvatica*	Europe	40 (640)	Pinkish red to yellow-brown	European Beech has a close even texture. It is a strong wood but hard to work. It is used for bench tops, tool handles, and for the framework of upholstered furniture.
6)	Beech, Silver	*Nothofagus menziesii*	New Zealand	36 (580)	Pinkish brown	Silver Beech is straight-grained. It has a fine, even texture and a lustrous surface.
7)	Birch, Silver or White Birch	*Betula pendula*	Scandinavia	41 (650)	White to light brown	This wood has a fairly straight grain, a fine texture, but a plain appearance.
8)	Birch, Yellow	*Betula lutea*	Eastern Canada and USA	45 (720)	Light to dark reddish brown	Yellow Birch has a variable grain, but a fine, even texture.
9)	Black Bean	*Castanospermum australe*	Queensland and New South Wales, Australia	44 (710)	Chocolate brown with lighter markings	Black Bean is a decorative wood with a greasy nature. It can have the appearance of Queensland Walnut.

SOME SUITABLE HARDWOODS

COMMON NAME	BOTANICAL NAME	ORIGIN	WEIGHT LB/FT³ (KG/M³)	COLOR	COMMENT
10) Blackwood	*Acacia melanoxylon*	New South Wales, Victoria, and Tasmania, Australia	41 (660)	Golden brown to dark brown	Blackwood is usually straight-grained, but it can be fiddle-back.
11) Cedar	*Cedrela mexicana*	Honduras and Brazil	30 (480)	Red to reddish brown	This is the scented cigar-box cedar. Do not confuse this species with Western Red Cedar. This wood can be used for the bottoms of drawers.
12) Cherry	*Prunus serotina*	Eastern Canada and USA	30 (480)	White to light reddish brown	Cherry has a moderately fine and even texture.
13) Chestnut, Sweet or Spanish Chestnut	*Castanea sativa*	Europe	35 (560)	Yellow-brown	This wood resembles English Oak. It works and finishes well, but it is rather soft.
14) Coach-wood or Scented Satinwood	*Ceratopetalum apetalum*	New South Wales, Australia	39 (620)	Light pinkish brown	This wood has a pleasant appearance, a distinctive scent, and a smooth silky finish from planing.

No.	Name	Botanical name	Origin	Weight	Colour	Description
15)	Elm, Common	*Ulmus procera*	Europe	35 (560)	Light brown	This is the tree that has been ravaged by disease. It is a handsome wood with a distinctive grain pattern. It cannot be split easily with a chisel.
16)	Elm, Japanese	*Ulmus*: various	Japan	39 (620)	Light brown	This wood is similar to Common Elm but it is milder and more stable.
17)	Freijo	*Cordia goeldiana*	Brazil	37 (590)	Light yellow with frequent golden brown streaks	Freijo has a moderately coarse, uneven texture and a spicy smell. It is strong and works well, and could occasionally be used as a substitute for Teak.
18)	Gum, Red or Satin Walnut	*Liquidambar styraciflua*	Southeastern USA	35 (560)	Brown or reddish brown with dark streaks	This wood has a very fine, even texture.
19)	Idigbo or Emeri or Black Afara	*Terminalia ivorensis*	West Africa	36 (580)	Pale lemon to light brown	This wood has a uniform grain and texture and a moderately lustrous surface. It is stable and works well.
20)	*Iroko	*Chlorophora excelsa*	Tropical Africa	41 (660)	Yellow toning to golden brown	Iroko has a medium-coarse texture, a fairly handsome grain pattern, and a moderately lustrous surface. In some ways it resembles Teak. It can be used indoors and outdoors.

SOME SUITABLE HARDWOODS

COMMON NAME	BOTANICAL NAME	ORIGIN	WEIGHT LB/FT³ (KG/M³)	COLOR	COMMENT
21) Jarrah	*Eucalyptus marginata*	Western Australia	51 (820)	Reddish brown, darkening	The grain can be straight or interlocked. The texture is medium-coarse and even. This is a durable wood.
22) *Mahogany, African or Khaya	*Khaya ivorensis*	West Africa	35 (560)	Medium red, slowly darkening	This wood has a medium-coarse texture, and it can have an interlocked grain which is attractive—but difficult to plane. It has a lustrous surface and polishes excellently. It is available in wide boards.
23) Mahogany, Brazilian	*Swietenia:* various	Brazil	34 (540)	Yellow to deep rich brown	Brazilian Mahogany was the original furniture-making Mahogany. It is almost the same as Honduras Mahogany.
24) *Mahogany, Honduras or Cuban Mahogany	*Swietenia macrophylia*	Central and South America	34 (540)	Yellow to deep rich brown	This is a very stable wood, and is easily worked. It finishes well, and can be used both indoors and outdoors.
25) *Makore or Cherry Mahogany	*Mimusops heckelii*	West Africa	46 (740)	Reddish brown with dark streaks	This wood is neither a true Cherry nor a true Mahogany. It is heavier than Mahogany and of a finer texture.

No. / Name	Botanical name	Origin	Weight	Colour	Notes
26) *Mansonia	*Mansonia altissima*	West Africa	39 (620)	Purple-brown	Mansonia is a fairly hard wood, usually straight-grained and with a smooth texture. It is sometimes used as a substitute for Walnut.
27) Maple, Queensland or Silkwood	*Flindersia brayleyana*	Queensland, Australia	34 (540)	Pinkish brown, darkening to medium brown	This wood has an interlocked or wavy grain that is sometimes marked with ripples. It has a mild pleasant smell. It polishes well.
28) Meranti	*Shorea:* various	Malaya	35 (560)	Light-red and dark-red varieties	Meranti has a course texture and a fairly uniform color. It is sometimes used as a substitute for Mahogany.
29) Myrtle or Myrtle Beech	*Nothofagus cunninghamii*	Victoria and Tasmania, Australia	45 (720)	Pinkish brown	This wood works well and takes a good polish.
30) Oak, Canadian	*Quercus:* various	Canada and USA	42 (670)	White and red varieties	White Oak is preferred to Red Oak.
31) Oak, European	*Quercus robur*	Europe	45 (720)	Creamy yellow	European Oak is strong and durable, and has an attractive ray figure. It was at one time the traditional wood for furniture construction.
32) Oak, Japanese	*Quercus mongolica*	Japan	42 (670)	Golden yellow-brown	Japanese Oak is more stable than European Oak, but is not as attractive. It's suitable for furniture construction, but not for exterior work.

SOME SUITABLE HARDWOODS

COMMON NAME	BOTANICAL NAME	ORIGIN	WEIGHT LB/FT³ (KG/M³)	COLOR	COMMENT
33) Oak, Silky	*Cardwellia sublimis*	Queensland Australia	38 (610)	Pinkish brown, darkening	Silky Oak has a silky luster and it shows an attractive ray figure when quarter-sawn.
34) Oak, Tasmanian or Mountain Ash, or Eucalyptus	*Eucalyptus:* various	Australia and Tasmania	44 (710)	Pinkish brown to light brown, darkening	This wood is straight-grained, moderately hard, but fairly easy to work. It has no characteristic taste or smell.
35) Sapele	*Entandrophragma cylindricum*	West Africa	40 (640)	Typical mahogany	Sapele has an interlocking grain giving it a ribbon stripe effect: This makes it difficult to plane. Sapele is harder than African Mahogany.
36) Sycamore	*Acer pseudoplatanus*	Europe	38 (610)	Milky white toning to golden yellow	Sycamore works well. It is tasteless, so is used when wood has to be in contact with food. It is also used for drawer sides and for the backs of cabinets.
37) *Teak	*Tectona grandis*	Burma, India, and Thailand	40 (640)	Golden yellow-brown, darkening. It sometimes has dark streaks.	Teak is strong, stable, and resistant to moisture, fire and acid. It can be used indoors and outdoors. It's greasy nature makes it hard to glue.

No.	Name	Botanical Name	Weight	Colour	Source	Characteristics
38)	Utile	*Entandrophragma utile*	42 (670)	Uniform red or purplish brown	West Africa	This is a popular hardwood and one that is easily obtained. Utile is closely related to Sapele, but the former is more stable and easier to work. Utile is used by the furniture industry for making drawer sides.
39)	Walnut, African or Nigerian Walnut, or Tigerwood, or Lovoa-wood	*Lovoa klaineana*	35 (560)	Golden brown with thin black streaks	West Africa	This wood has a medium-coarse texture and a lustrous surface. It sometimes has an interlocked grain. It is not a true Walnut, but is sometimes used as a substitute.
40)	Walnut, American Black	*Juglans nigra*	39 (620)	Rich, dark purple-brown	Central USA	American Black Walnut works well and polishes well. It is used for high-class work.
41)	Walnut, Queensland or Australian Laurel or Australian Walnut	*Endiandra palmerstonii*	46 (740)	Darkish brown with grayish green to black stripes	Queensland, Australia	This wood has an unpleasant smell when freshly cut. It has a lustrous surface when planed, but can be difficult to saw. It is used mainly as a highly decorative veneer.
42)	Whitewood or Yellow Poplar	*Liriodendron tulipifera*	32 (520)	Light to dark yellow or pinkish brown	Southern USA	This wood has a straight grain and a fairly fine, even texture.

Glossary

BACKSAW—A hand tool used for cutting tenons. It has a reinforced back edge and finer teeth than either the crosscut saw or rip saw.

BANDSAW—A machine tool that is used for cutting wood up to six inches thick, and for making straight or curved cuts in any materials.

BELT SANDER—A portable machine tool that is used to sand furniture and cabinetwork. This type of sander has an abrasive belt that can be changed easily.

BENCH DOG—A piece of wood or metal that projects through the top of a woodworking bench and prevents the wood from flying off the top of the bench when one side is planed.

BRAD—A slender nail that has a small, deep head.

CENTER PUNCH—A hand tool that is used to accurately position holes in wood.

CHIPBOARD SCREW—A screw used primarily in chipboard because it grips better than the ordinary type of screw and is less likely to split the wood.

CLAMP—A hand tool used to hold woodwork together on the bench, and also for holding small pieces of wood together while the glue between the pieces sets.

CONTACT ADHESIVE—Emulsions or solutions of natural or synthetic rubbers that are generally used for sticking plastic laminate to blockboard or chipboard, but which can also be used for sticking wood, cork, rubber, metal, leather and ceramics.

COPING SAW—A hand tool used for making curved cuts in wood less than an inch thick.

CORK BLOCK—A hand tool used to grip abrasive paper.

CUTTING GAUGE—A hand tool used to mark on the wood one line that has to be across the grain of the wood and parallel to one end of the wood. It is frequently used when marking out a dovetail joint.

DOVETAIL SAW—A hand tool with fine teeth that is used for cutting dovetails.

DOWEL JOINT—The simplest of all joints, it is used in the mass production of furniture, and is held together with nails, screws, or corner blocks.

END RABBET JOINT—A joint that is used generally on boxes. It creates a large gluing surface and helps woodworkers locate the parts accurately.

EPOXY RESIN—A strong glue that is used in small quantities to fix ceramic, glass, metal, rubber and wood.

FIBREBOARD—A building material made of wood fibres compressed into rigid sheets.

FLAT-BOTTOM SPOKESHAVE—A tool used for removing convex shapes, and slightly concave shapes.

FLATHEAD SCREW—A screw used on even surfaces.

GRINDING—The coarse removal of metal.

HARDWOOD—Hard, compact wood that is difficult to cut. Hardwoods usually are deciduous, and are generally used in furniture making.

JACK PLANE—A hand tool used to plane a very flat surface. Though its controls are identical to those of a smoothing plane, it is longer.

JOINTING—The process of levelling teeth on a saw by running a flat file along the point of the teeth until each tooth has a small flat area where the point should be.

MACHINE PLANER—A machine tool that planes, and also cuts rabbets, chamfers, and tapered shapes. It is generally used to produce a smooth finish on one side of the work.

MARKING GAUGE—A hand tool used in the planing of lumber. It is used to mark on the wood one line that is parallel to the edge of the wood, and marks only with the direction of the grain.

MARKING KNIFE—A hand tool used to mark a line across the wood at the place where accurate sawing has to be done.

MORTISE-AND-TENON JOINT—A joint formed when an accurately made tenon on the end of one piece of wood fits into a mortise cut into the second piece.

MORTISE-AND-TENON WITH DADO—A joint that is used for the upright division of a cabinet.

MORTISE GAUGE—A hand tool used to mark on the wood two lines that are parallel to the edge of the wood, and which marks only with the direction of the grain. It is frequently used when marking out a mortise-and-tenon joint.

MORTISING MACHINE—A machine tool that rapidly and accurately cuts mortises—rectangular slots—in any type of wood.

OILSTONE—A hand tool used for sharpening chisels and plane blades.

PLOW PLANE—A hand tool used for making grooves, rabbets and tongues. It has 10 cutters of different widths.

POLYVINYL ACETATE—This glue, which comes in a squeeze tube and sets fairly rapidly, is better known as PVA.

RABBET PLANE—A hand tool that has a blade as wide as its body, and which can be used for trimming directly against an edge, and for trimming the rabbets of joints.

RADIAL ARM SAW—A machine with a revolving vertical spindle and cutter for milling out the surface of the wood or metal.

SABER SAW—A portable electric saw that can cut either straight or curved paths in wood.

SECRET HAUNCHED MORTISE-AND-TENON JOINT—A joint that is used between the leg and the rail on a stool.

SHOOTING BOARD—A workshop aid that supports the wood when the end grain is planed.

SMOOTHING PLANE—A hand tool used for shaping wood and for preparing wood to a smooth surface that is ready for polishing.

SOFTWOOD—A wood that is easily cut. Softwoods, usually evergreens, are commonly used for structural and painted work.

THROUGH DOVETAIL JOINT—A strong corner joint that is also decorative, and which can also be used on cabinets.

TRY SQUARE—A hand tool that is used for making right angle cuts across wood.

UPHOLSTERY—The trade of padding furniture with fabric and springs.

UREA FORMALDEHYDE—A waterproof glue that is better known by the trade names of Cascamite and Aerolite.

Index

lamps
  adjustable standard, 99–101, 102
  table, 86, 87–91, 92
locks, 54, 56

M

machine planer, 30, 31–32, 33
  safety procedures for, 60
machine tools
  advantages and disadvantages of, 24
  stand for, 38, 39
machine tools, types of, 24–39
  bandsaw, 25, 26–27
  belt sander, 37, 38
  electric drill, 33, 34
  machine planer, 30, 31–32, 33
  mortising machine, 35, 36
  radial arm saw, 28–29, 30
  saber saw, 36, 37
magnetic catches, 53, 54
mallet, 17
marking gauge, 15
marking knife, 14, 43
miter box, 14, 74, 75
mortise-and-tenon joint, 44, 45, 46
  secret haunched, 47
  square haunched, 46, 47
  with dado, 47, 48, 49
mortise chisel, 17
mortise gauge, 15
mortises, 35
mortising machine, 35, 36

N

nail set, 15
needle, upholstery, 58, 59

O

oilstone, 17
oilstone case, 70, 71, 72

P

piano hinge, 53, 54
picture-frame screw eyes, 54, 56
picture framing, 84, 85, 86
plane blades, sharpening, 17, 18–19, 20
planes, 16

playhouse, 81–83, 84
plow plane, 16
polishes, 51, 52
polishing rubber, 51, 52
polyurethane varnish, 52
polyvinyl acetate, 52
projects
  adjustable standard lamps, 99–101, 102
  briefcase, 92–93
  carver chair, 128, 129–134, 135
  corner cupboard, 94–98
  fireside chairs, 123, 124–127, 128
  formica-top table, 106, 107–109, 110
  kitchen cupboard, 94–98
  picture framing, 84, 85, 86
  playhouse, 81–83, 84
  recliner, 135, 136–145, 146
  sideboard, 146, 147–153
  table lamps, 86, 87–91, 92
  television table, 110, 111–114
  tile-top table, 102, 103–105, 106
  toy tractor, 79, 80
  toy van, 76–78, 79
PVA glue, *see* polyvinyl acetate

R

rabbet plane, 16
radial arm saw, 28–29, 30
recliner, 135, 136–145, 146
reconstituted foam, 58
resource centers, 156
ripsawing, 29
roofing nails, 57
router, 16
rubber webbing, 57, 58
ruler, 14
rusting, 38, 39

S

saber saw, 36
saws
  safety procedures for, 60, 61
  sharpening, 20, 21, 22
  types of, 13, 36, 37
screw cover-heads, 53, 54
screwdriver, 15
screw eyes, picture-frame, 54, 56
screws, 53, 54, 56
seasoning, 40
seat span, 57

Acknowledgments

The author and publisher wish to thank Mr. S. T. Williams for his skilled editorial advice on the manuscript. Thanks also to Mrs. Hill, who typed the manuscript in a thorough and craftsmanlike manner.